In The Shadow Of
The Cotton Tree

"Identity"

In The Shadow Of The Cotton Tree

A Diary of Second World War Sierra Leone

Jack Rillie

with a
Foreword by Andrew Hook
and an
Afterword by Marshall Walker

Edited by Alasdair Soussi

"The cotton tree drops its leaves, today it is bare,
tomorrow or the next day it will be clotted with green again."
Jack Rillie, Freetown, 1941

Mansion Field

Mansion Field
An imprint of Zeticula Ltd
The Roan,
Kilkerran,
KA19 8LS
Scotland

http://www.mansionfield.co.uk

First published in 2014

ISBN 978-1-905021-13-0

For my parents,
Judith Anne Marena Soussi
(Jack's elder daughter),
and Ahmad Chafic Soussi.
Thank you. For everything.
Alasdair

Jack, Gold Coast, c. 1944-45

Alert. Midnight.

Great God! the sluice of fire
the guns vomit into darkness
and screen the sky where once
the star-fires dimly pulsed!
Is the raider-scaring dawn
skulking too
in the earthly shelter of the hills?
Again alert, and Fear
rides the switchback Siren,
the acid smell of it taints the air
of cellarage and sandbagged passageway.
In a hump-backed shelter
an old man sits with aspen underlip
and bones rattling like loose shutters
in the wind's bluster; the candle shadows
in tattered-scarecrow-rags
flap silently about his shoulders.
His cupped frame
jealously hoards
the treasure of his eighty years
and he wraps his memories round him
like an old brocaded cloak
as he hears broadcast
the elaborate palaver
of Death's approach.
A mother buckles her soul
to a lullaby
and young men in love
watch Hate
stalking the skies,
prowling and snouting
in urban corridors
and slavering on altar steps.
Hope is depth-charged here,
all the masonry of dreams
is bombed and only
the swift undertow of life
is tugging at the living heart.

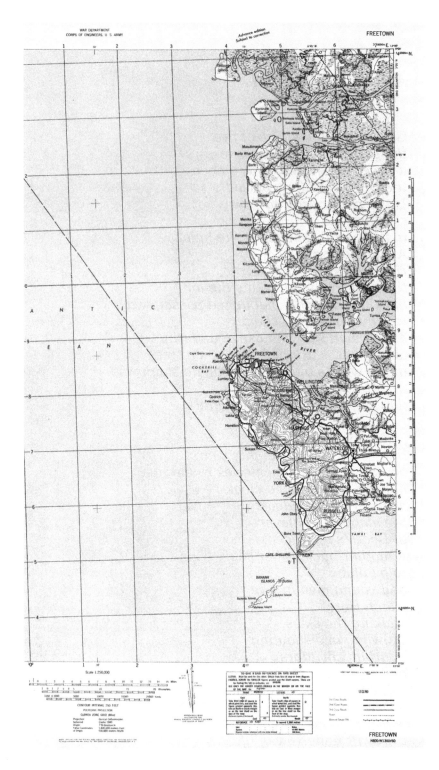

U.S. Army Map Service, Freetown, 1942

viii

Contents

List of Illustrations

Foreword

When I took up an appointment in English Literature at Glasgow University in 1979, Jack Rillie, the head of the department, was within a few years of retirement. Very much the department's elder statesman, he was a charismatic figure, elegantly embodying its fine tradition of teaching the great works of English Literature to successive generations of Glasgow students. How different his situation had been when not yet 23 years old, and in a world utterly remote from the Victorian splendours of Gilmorehill, he had lectured on Shakespeare for the very first time.

Born in 1918, near the end of the First World War, Jack was a student at Glasgow when the Second World War began. In no time at all he found himself serving in the Royal Army Medical Corps. In 1940, newly married to Betty, he was posted to – of all unlikely places – the African city of Freetown in Sierra Leone. Sixteen months were to pass before he was able to leave West Africa and return to the United Kingdom. It is this period of exile that the material, published here for the first time, brings vividly to life. Keeping a diary, and writing occasional poems, clearly helped Jack to cope with the depressingly exotic circumstances in which he found himself.

From the beginning Jack makes it clear that he hated both the army and the war. He came to accept that the war was necessary: fascism had to be defeated. But he never changed his view of the hopeless incompetence of the British Army and the way it was run. The British Navy (which had got him safely from the Clyde to Freetown) and the R.A.F. (which was winning the Battle of Britain) he admired. But the bungling army was one long endurance test. Nor did he ever feel that his and his colleagues' presence in remote West Africa was contributing anything of significance to the winning of the war. Thousands of miles away from any kind of action, most of the time he seems to have felt only the pointlessness of his African isolation. Even civilians back in the U.K., having to endure Luftwaffe bombing raids, were contributing more to the war effort.

Freetown itself proved to have nothing to offer the exiled soldier. Seen from a distance, the city might have some romantic appeal. But in reality it was, as Jack put it, "like a leper clothed in purple and gold." It was ugly, hot and squalid, with fetid, congested streets, and jerry-built houses. Its impoverished native inhabitants – no better off, according to Jack, than "freed slaves" – were casually exploited by foreign outsiders. Jack summed up Freetown as a "tropical mausoleum". Hence it is hardly a surprise to learn that his long months there had decidedly few redeeming features. There were occasional lively debates with fellow-soldiers on such topics as the kind of Britain that would emerge from the war. Jack reports that one of his colleagues held political views that were "a deep shade of pink", and he comments presciently: "if we are all possessed of the same energy and bitterness as he after the war we will have a new country and a new government." Then there was the opportunity that the future lecturer in English Literature had to get on with his reading. Near the diary's end he provides a fascinating list of all the books he had been able to read. (What is striking is how English-centred the list is: Scottish and American authors make only rare appearances). But just as I myself benefited from the reading opportunity provided by National Service in West Germany some 15 years later, so Jack must sometimes have been grateful for the reading he got through in Sierra Leone when he began his post-war teaching career at Glasgow University.

Another good time emerged when the future lecturer was put in charge of the hospital library. Jack writes vividly about how this change raised his spirits. Away from the daily grind of the hospital wards, he felt re-energised, even thinking again about writing plans of his own. And by an even better stroke of luck, there was a brief period when he found himself lecturing on Shakespeare to students at Fourah Bay College in Freetown: his very first experience of university teaching. But for me at least, what this diary reveals above all is that what kept Jack Rillie sane – and able to endure the boredom and emptiness, the sense of isolation and alienation, the meaninglessness of his life in distant West Africa – was his overwhelming love for his wife Betty. He lived for her letters – and the unfailing dream of their continuing life together. Marriage to Betty made Jack's life. More than anything else, that is what we learn from this diary, which now, more than 70 years after it was written, we are all able to read and enjoy.

Andrew Hook
Glasgow
June 2014

Introduction

I tried to imagine what my grandfather would have made of my travelling to Sierra Leone as I touched down at Freetown's Lungi International Airport one humid October evening at the close of the country's rainy season. As I looked out towards the darkness beyond, and my muscles tightened in anticipation of what was to come, my thoughts turned towards him and his time in this small West African nation, which, from the very moment he set foot upon its sun-scorched earth as a wide-eyed 22-year-old, would forever imprint itself on his consciousness. His 16-month stint in what was then a British colony fighting for King and Country during the Second World War was not an experience filled with the true "horrors" of war, but, in so many other ways, it was no less challenging.

Even as a very young boy, and way before I understood any notions of war and serving one's country, I was always aware of his "adventures" in Africa through the many mementos that adorned his and my grandmother Betty's elegant red sand-stone property in Glasgow's west-end. And, of course, his many anecdotes, which, often tinged with black humour, he would recall with near-perfect clarity right up until the end of his life. As I hit my teenage years, and drawn by a love of history, which, from Richard the Lionheart and Saladin to the grim horrors of the Great War and beyond, fascinated and captivated my otherwise frivolous young mind, I became enthralled by his tales of visiting tribes in the villages, his trips through the jungle and his general experiences of acting as a nursing orderly in the Royal Army Medical Corps (RAMC) in deepest, darkest Africa. From an early age I was also made aware of the various diseases, which one might contract in the tropics. Top of these were malaria, which is still a notorious killer in Africa today, and which I too encountered on my own visit to the land that Pedro da Cintra so colourfully bestowed the name of "Serra Lyoa" – or Lion Mountain – after the Portuguese navigator sailed past the mountainous Sierra Leone peninsula en route to India in 1462.

As I grew to understand the Second World War and its nuances, however, I began to realise just what a contribution the man known to his friends as Jack made, even if his was a less harrowing experience than that of many who served in the conflict's other warring theatres.

The ruins of old Fourah Bay College – constructed between 1845 and 1848 – in Cline Town, Freetown, today

By less harrowing, I mean largely unencumbered by the traditional sights and sounds of war, for Sierra Leone was not on the frontline of combat operations. Nonetheless, put on a ship in a grave time of conflict and transported some 3,000 miles away to an obscure African state in the Atlantic was, in itself, harrowing enough. So too the very real prospect of being torpedoed by a marauding German U-boat off the busy West African coast, not to mention the frequently sun-beaten, other times thunderous and rain-strewn 500 days that followed. This was a time when he came face-to-face with all manner of experiences, ranging from being buzzed by Nazi German warplanes to being asked by a fellow soldier for assistance in his novel (if slightly potty) escape bid, so desperate was he to flee the confines of war.

It was these memories and more besides that raced through my mind as I too set foot on this piece of West Africa, Graham Greene, through his pity-riddled policeman, Henry Scobie, labelled a most "unfashionable colony" in his Sierra Leone-based tale of love, tragedy and despair, The Heart of the Matter (1948).[1] As I breathed in the storm-soaked air of this diamond-rich but socially impoverished country for the first time, I did so a full seven-decades after Jack himself first anchored off Freetown harbour – and, perhaps, caught the same clingy odours of this coastal capital in his untrained nostrils – as an aspiring intellectual from the east-end of Glasgow, my journey to the same city having taken six hours as opposed to his 10 days. A brutal 10-year civil war that ended in 2002 between the government and the Revolutionary United Front (RUF) had battered modern-day Sierra Leone to a shattering degree: 50,000 killed, countless thousands left maimed and psychologically scarred by the RUF's terrifying drug and alcohol-induced penchant for amputating limbs and mass rape. It brought this already politically fragile nation, which welcomed some 30,000 mostly British and French visitors to its shores each year before the outbreak of war, to its knees as foreign investors fled, tourists dried-up and unemployment spiralled. Only now, and particularly with the April 26, 2012, conviction of former Liberian leader Charles Taylor, who was found guilty of aiding and abetting war crimes during the Sierra Leone civil war, is it slowly beginning to reassert itself as a peaceful and forward-thinking nation-state in this most colourful of continents.

Unlike Jack's time in Freetown, where, with his David Niven-esque good looks, he cut a dash in his British West African Army uniform (but revelled in very little besides), my visit to this one million-plus populated African capital was a fleeting one. But, using his war diary as a quasi-city

A street-level view of Freetown's legendary Cotton Tree

guide, I made my own way across its many pot-holed streets, lanes and thoroughfares to see the areas, which he had recorded all those years ago for myself. And, sure enough, there they were, some described in such detail by Jack that I was astonished to see little had changed. There were the likes of Mount Aureol, which, overlooking the east end of the city, then hosted the British Military Hospital to which he was posted shortly after his arrival; Wilberforce in the west, to where he was subsequently transferred; and Fourah Bay College – the early 19th century-established institution once situated in Cline Town, in Freetown's deprived eastern quarter, now itself atop Mount Aureol – where Jack spent some of his war service teaching English Literature to local students, and where he would cut his teeth as a prelude to a then undetermined future career as a distinguished academic in the lecture rooms of Glasgow University. Mentioned in rich detail in his diary, these landmarks were all accessible during a day's taxi ride across Freetown's frequently log-jammed streets, which, gloriously titled Newcastle Street, Regent Street, Walpole Street and such like, proclaimed Sierra Leone's strong British credentials. (It won its independence in 1961 but required British military support to help end the carnage of its civil war). My exploration of the city was not complete, however, until I gazed upon its mighty cotton tree, an ancient and revered landmark in the heart of the capital. This was in existence in 1787 when British philanthropists founded the "Province of Freedom" along the estuary of the Sierra Leone River, and under its boughs a group of former black slaves, who had won their liberty by fighting with the British in the American War of Independence, are said to have gathered in 1792 to praise God for their deliverance as founders of the newly established settlement of Freetown.

While the significance of British West Africa (the Gambia, the Gold Coast, Nigeria and Sierra Leone) in the Second World War might not be overly apparent today, back then its role was clear, playing, as it did, an integral part in the Allied war effort against Nazi Germany. Aircraft heading for the Middle East and the North African front flew via West Africa, while eastern-bound ships, unable to traverse the waters of the Suez Canal and forced to sail the more lengthy Cape of Good Hope, were serviced at West African ports. Freetown itself, where an estimated excess of 10,000 British troops were stationed between 1939 and 1945, was of great strategic importance, with its natural harbour and mountain ranges providing both the British Navy and Air Force with a crucial footing for the war in the South Atlantic. Up to 150 ships could be accommodated into its

A street scene of Second World War Freetown, November 7, 1942

well-protected harbour, and, in less than two years during wartime, the population of Freetown, which served as the headquarters for both the Royal Navy and Royal Air Force in West Africa, doubled in size as tens of thousands of men laboured on construction sites and the docks or were enlisted into military units. And again, while not a combat zone, Sierra Leone was surrounded by the threatening spectre of French West Africa, which, after the French military defeat to the Germans in 1940, had declared for the Nazi-collaborationist Vichy regime of Marshal Philippe Pétain, who, as well as governing the unoccupied areas of southern France, established control over the colonies that made up the extensive Gallic empire.

In one sense, then, Jack, who came close to sharing his wartime service in Freetown with the prolific Greene who, from 1942 to 1943, worked in the murkier world of British intelligence, was just another small cog in the gigantic wheel that was the British Army fighting the globally consuming conflict known as the Second World War. Yet, by virtue of his diary, he contributed so much more. So, what fuels my desire to publish his account of his time in Freetown from August 1940 to December 1941 now is three-fold: on a personal level, my natural instinct leads me to the opinion that his writings are far too important to be left to simply gather dust; on a historical level, they offer the reader an intriguing insight into a part of the conflict rarely featured in today's retrospective accounts of the Second World War; but crucially, publishing provides an invaluable opportunity to showcase the early writings of a man who would go on to be the unsung hero of much of Scotland's thriving literary scene. Here, as a quiet, thoughtful, yet hugely admired and influential academic figure in the English Literature department of his beloved Glasgow University where he worked for more than 40 years, he would be a guiding influence behind some of Scotland's most celebrated writers, such as William McIlvanney, author of the critically acclaimed novel, Docherty, Archie Hind, the creator of the seminal Glasgow work, The Dear Green Place, and Hugh C. Rae, who found fame with his nom de plume, Jessica Stirling.

Indeed, as I write these words, it seems extraordinary to me that a man with the intellect that Jack so possessed never published a book of his own during his considerable lifetime. The reasons for this are unimportant here, but that he was more committed to teaching and to his students than ambition is, as many of his friends and colleagues would testify, part of his academic legacy. Barring some elements of editing – mostly for purposes of clarity, to protect the identity of some individuals concerned and to concentrate its more diffuse elements – the following represents a faithful rendition of Jack's war diary (and leaves untouched any understandable inaccuracies of date and event). His own recollections of it and his life prior to war, written decades later while in his eighties and specially edited here – for the sole purposes of this book – into a brief introduction, "A Young Life Recalled", are also included.

In essence, the text of his diary – very literary in feel, and, I always imagine, written by the dim glow of candlelight as beads of sweat dripped irksomely from the end of his nose in Freetown's humid swell – is the candid thoughts, views and experiences of a gifted young man in a situation many of us would find intolerable. Bursting with the vocabulary of a would-be scholar still trying to find his own voice his prose is, at times, overwrought and, as he readily admitted himself, excessively grandiose, but rarely does it disappoint. As such, and together with many stunning examples of his contemporaneous war poetry (derived from both his diary and a second book in which he collated much of his war-time verse), it is an altogether expressive, outspoken, sometimes raw and uncomfortable account of a bygone age, which is the product, and sole product, of John Archibald McKenzie Rillie.

Alasdair Soussi
Glasgow
June 2014

For My Grandmother

So you are alone and lonely now, my dear?
Alone with the promise of snow in a grey sky,
In a dead winter. Fretting with dry hands
At the heavy curtains, knowing the desertion
And shuttered hopelessness of the upstairs room,
Gazing at the spent garden and the bare woods
Where all night long the owl's call
Haunts the dreaming of your little sleeps.
A year today. He who had been tender
And kind to you for forty years. Cruel,
Cruel darling. His studs on the dressing table,
His coat behind the door and the children gone
And the grandchildren who never met you,
Never arranged your shawls or rocked your chair.
They will not recognise the secret splendours
Of your blood in them nor know the wise
Care you gave our fathers. But your ways
Are unforgotten and the feet of the unseen child
Follow still. The past puts out its buds.
You would not wish, I think, another year
To bear with dimming eyes and failing powers
The gainless gathering in of hours and days.
Go now, dear heart, before the spring
Wakes in you the fadeless years of his love.

A Young Life Recalled

I was born in Dailly, Ayrshire, on June 1, 1918. The first five-and-a-half years of my life were spent in a small "suburb" of the village – "Romilly". It was a group of perhaps a dozen small houses between a forest to the north and the Glasgow-Stranraer railway to the south. Away to the west was a long-disused brickyard and to the east, the winding-gear of the near-expended Maxwell Pit. Here, I learned about tree felling from the woodcutters in the forest – and about badgers, which had setts and young. These visits – uphill – were on my father's shoulders. I occasionally fell into deepish drains in the old brickyard and had to be rescued. My aversion to water dates from this childhood trauma.

My first connection with history was here. The notorious Black and Tans, sent to suppress the Irish revolution, went past our house in trains heading for Stranraer – and the Irish boat. We waved to them and sometimes got a tammy in return! But, they weren't a great success in Ireland. Post-1918, I was, of course, born into a shattered country, but a child's awareness is simply of what is the case. War is stories – uncles', neighbours' stories of trenches, of "over-the-top", of the noise of gun-fire, of attacking – there is romance in the blood and dirt – "tell me about the war". My father talked little of it – an electrical engineer for South Ayrshire Collieries, he was in a protected occupation. I can, in retrospect, see some embarrassment in his reluctance. Some of my fellow pupils had no fathers. Only much later would I be shown their names on the memorial. The Black and Tans who waved from troop-trains were – as mentioned – exciting for us.

I had to leave in 1929 when my family moved to Glasgow. My father had found employment in Airdrie and returned home to Dailly for weekends. Then with the help

A proud Jack sporting his school uniform, aged 10-11

of his brother, Ben, we got a house to rent in Dennistoun in Bathgate Street where Ben and his family had lived for some time. It was a typical Glasgow street of grey stone tenements. I was genuinely scared I'd never be able to find my home if I left. There were numbers on the closes. Suppose you forgot the number? Then, I was not going to the nearest local school. It was "rough". Alexandra Parade Primary School was "respectable". It was a big red stone imposing school with three levels, high ornate iron railings and vast playgrounds. And, it seemed, far away from home, crossing a busy road, turning right, then left, up a long hill of identical flats. Somebody took me. Somebody else brought me home, and pointed out, "See! Number 48!" After a week of sitting in a classroom amongst strangers and worrying about the way home, I was convinced it was possible.

Unforeseen, however, was the language barrier. I was never quite sure what the natives were saying. They looked at me as if I spoke funny. In class, in that first week, I was as passive as I could be. The old boy who taught us, at some juncture, when the class was silent to his question, asked, "You, John Riley, new boy – do you know?"

"Yes, I ken," says I, pleased to be noticed.

After that he'd say, "we'll ask John if he 'kens'". He got a titter. I noticed everybody said, "you know", always said, "yes" for "aye", didn't understand "fer feochan". So I learned Glasgow English – only to discover at my next school that that too was vulgar.

Whitehill Secondary School was several gears up. It was large. The teachers all wore gowns. There were plaques in the hall – one a memorial for the 1914-18 war, the other a list entitled, Dux. Two fearsome janitors. A football ground. A gymnasium. In my second year, and still a vulnerable country yokel, I caught diphtheria and spent six weeks in complete isolation – even from my parents – in Belvidere Hospital. I had to lie flat on my back for three weeks. I really didn't feel very ill. But, they let me out at the end of my six weeks, and I was then off school for a

Jack's parents, David and Peg, probably standing outside their old house in Dailly, c.1939

while and really couldn't do the exams. So, I repeated second year and that wasted year I always felt forever kept me back – slowed me down. But, I got to edit the school magazine in 1937, managed some prizes and left that year with English, Maths, Latin and Greek Highers. I don't remember much discussion about the matter at home, but if I got the grants, and perhaps a bursary from the university competition, I'd go to university.

I looked forward to the end of the vacation but went, dutifully and unsuspectingly, with my parents and my friend, David Symers, to Dunoon, on the Cowal Coast. We walked past Dunoon Pier towards the West Bay alert for suitable companionship and got as far as the tennis courts. There was a girl "waving" a racquet. To attract us? No way! We waved ourselves over and introduced ourselves. Met the awaited tennis partner. Asked if we could watch their game. Reluctantly they agreed. We chatted after their game, explored our pockets, suggested the next day's Kyles of Bute Cruise – by paddle steamer. It was a date. Leaving them, David suggested that we toss for a partner. I agreed. Before we met, however, I had made up my mind. No toss up. David didn't care. We met the girls on Dunoon Pier. A bit of confusion as David walked onto the pier beside my date. Some surprise on the girl's faces as we swapped. We sailed up the Kyles and back. I knew. Her name was Betty Scorah, her address 321 Alderman Road, Knightswood, Glasgow.She worked in an insurance office in town. Our first date in town was under the Tramway Clock at the junction of Renfield Street and Bath Street. We continued to date for the next two-and-a-half years.

My first year at the University of Glasgow passed uneventfully. We had little money – we walked to the university and back most days. But, as 1938 proceeded Germany was busy building her army – doubling the air-power of Britain. Appeasement was keeping fascism at bay – allowing Hitler to have his way with Austria, Mussolini with Abyssinia. By the time I was into my second year at university, there were air-raid precautions and increasing

Betty and Jack, August 1938, Dunoon

certainty about war. I, meanwhile, with some Labour friends, had gone along with the Peace Pledge Movement.[2] We attended meetings addressed by Bertrand Russell, Dick Sheppard (the Anglican canon) and Maude Royden. There was a lot of discussion amongst students. I was getting closer to the point of view that we could not stop war and if it came, not to enlist was to refuse to share the dangers – and the guilt (if that's what it was) – with those who fought. David Symers and I went down to Pollokshields to the Cameronians' HQ. They took us in, told us they had their complement, but there was an RAMC unit upstairs looking for recruits. That sounded good enough. We took the King's shilling. The following week we were kitted out in ill-fitting tunics with brass buttons, puttees and boots. Ghastly. We had to attend drill sessions – I think only weekly at first – but drill for over 100 amateur soldiers in that confined space was practically impossible. We had lectures/seminars on army regulations, on bandaging and splints. It was not taxing.

In the summer of 1938 we had to go to camp – Berwick-upon-Tweed – near the famous KOSB barracks whence came Reveille on a bugle every morning. One really felt ready for battle at that point! Breakfast, porridge on a tin plate, tea in a tin cup, reduced one's martial instincts. Berwick-upon-Tweed was attractive. There we went to a pub and there I had my first beer. We were smoking already. We were soldiers now!

Prime Minister Neville Chamberlain claimed he had seen Hitler off by the Munich Agreement in September 1938 at the cost of "that faraway country" Czechoslovakia. So, we had the prospect of getting back to our university second year in October. It was English Literature, Moral Philosophy – and a serious bout of English Language from Ritchie Girvan in the famous Kelvin lecture room with Kelvin's experiment on liquids still on the wall. It was a very fraught time politically, and increasingly the conviction spread that there would be war. We did drills and learned about gas-masks. There must have been a holiday in the summer of 1939. It would be Kirn, Dunoon, and I think Betty was there.

Jack and Betty, August 5, 1939, Dunoon

We were called up for duty and quartered in the (dry) Pollokshields Baths at the end of August. Hitler was out for Poland. We were filling sandbags to put round the university quadrangle. We listened to Chamberlain's solemn (if reluctant) declaration of war in the Baths on September 3. We were then posted to war quarters in St Augustine's Primary School, Coatbridge. There Betty visited some evenings. Then, on the banks of the canal, we got ourselves engaged! The ring was not expensive. I was on 7/- per week from His Majesty.

We were moved to Innerleithen, Peebles, in November. Then, in January 1940, we moved south to Dorset – to the cute, beautiful village of Beaminster – then later Aldershot where we were under canvas in a smallish field. The extraordinary feature of it was that in the night the whole field enclosed us along its hedges in a necklace of glow-worms. These countless steady little stars formed round us a kind of terrestrial constellation that needed no poetry to raise it onto some level of the spiritual. The only other worthwhile incident of our short delay there was the visit – after, apparently, a great harangue from the Guard Commander – of John Kellett, a man from Forres who had been one of our friends in those first two university years – now serving with the HLI, and now, like us, waiting for Europe.

At Aldershot, we made orderly ranks along the station. The train came in. We dumped our heavy kit in the guard's van and got aboard. The staff sergeant came up the platform shouting the names of "Rillie", "Symers" and "X". We disembarked, and were informed we had to go to a WOSB (selection for officer training). That, if sudden and confusing, seemed just fine – we'd heard that the Nazis had broken the European line. We asked for our kit – "it would be sent back from Dover. No time now". The train moved off. The Military Police appeared and were rightly sceptical of our story. Papers? None. Name of unit? "Well, with the 52 (L) Div. on the way to Belgium". They put us in the back of a 15-cwt truck and took us to Crookham Barracks.

Meanwhile, a fortnight was passing. David and I and other unknowns were digging deep trenches around the perimeter of the camp. The weather was good – far about us there were vapour trails and the faint rattle of machine guns. Once, in the distance, a plane spiralled down, smoking. We'd heard about our Spitfires. And we'd heard reported from Winston Churchill that this was to be "their finest hour". The air battle would go on into September.

David was posted to a tank regiment in Norfolk. I was posted to Clevedon – near Bristol. There I met Cyril Packham, who was to become a permanent friend. Clevedon was a pleasant location – but they were taking us on a ship overseas. Forty-eight hours leave to come. It was – looking back now – an extraordinary decision to make. Certainly not a good deal for Betty. I phoned her. Can we get married? The answer – surprisingly – was simply "yes". I got on the train about July 24/25 and got to dark Glasgow. We went to the Congregational Church to find its pews filled by Jersey Island refugees! We became husband and wife. After one night at a large "dignified" hotel at Charing Cross, I caught an afternoon train back to Clevedon and watched Betty diminishing on Platform One, Glasgow Central Station. For the next few days, I phoned and we said goodbye. Then I didn't phone – for a YEAR-and-a-HALF.

It was early August 1940 when we entrained for Gourock. We embarked on HMS Canton (an old P&O liner). This turned out to be an Armed Merchant Cruiser whose job was to protect convoys – carry troops solo. We were alone – with eight 6-inch and two 3-inch guns. We were enlisted to act as gun-crew if we met hostile shipping. We carried the shells! We took a cunning route (if we were going east) – north towards Iceland, south-west towards Newfoundland, south towards South America, eastwards towards Africa. We called at Freetown, Sierra Leone. The bay had a lot of ships at anchor – destroyers, merchant etc.

We drank lime juice. Bought bananas from bumboats. We transferred to the SS Monarch of Bermuda – manifestly a pleasure craft, a luxury liner. Now stripped down, it would do for a Hulk in Great Expectations. We didn't move. Then we scrambled down a kind of rope mat to the ferry below. We were on a high slope covered with flowers (Azaleas – wonderful!) above Freetown. Our quarters were still not ready, so we were under canvas. In my tent was a Southern Irishman, known, not surprisingly, as Paddy. On our first morning, he undid the flap and stepped outside, held his arms up to heaven, and said: "B' all the saints 'at Holy, it's Resurrection Day and ahm first up!"

We lined up then – and ever after – for our quinine, the neat liquid, which, at first, was dreadful. Sometime later, tablets were invented, which gave one quinine painlessly and coloured one yellow! Despite the precautions, there was a lot of malaria – but fortunately M.T. malaria and so non-recurring (until the next bite!).

Oddly, most of my service there was as librarian. There was a large handsome hall used for lectures and Sunday Church – one of the rooms off was used for the library. The hospital was quite large and there was an Essex Regt. Battalion, Artillery, RASC, REME etc around. I had to see that the sick read books (the Red Cross had made – and continued – a pretty good contribution – and not by any means popular material). I had a (kind of) eight to five day, with an evening session of an hour. On Sunday, I was a kind of altar boy to a, my God, boring Padre. I read – a lot. I did a lot of scribbling – abortive stories, pretentious poems, kept a (pompous) diary going. And – off duty – on evenings and Sundays, drank a lot of Canadian lager, sang army songs, did a sing-a-long to Cyril Packham's sax, did occasional boat tours up river to the original Portuguese and British settlements, threw stones at the lungfish and visited the outlying villages of grass and corrugated iron. The whole area – town and country – was splattered with Irish surnames – O'Toole, Murphy, Daniel, Riley, Rourke, Muldoon. They'd had a lot of visitors from the seas. There was a good tennis court in the hospital compound, too.

But, my best experience was being invited to help out at Fourah Bay College – an internal college of Durham

University and giving B.A. Durham degrees. One of the English staff was on sick leave. I had to take on The Merchant of Venice and some Romantic poetry. The class, all African – the college served all of West Africa – said very little and took a lot of notes (more than I could imagine worthwhile). I had a very genteel afternoon tea with china cups and cucumber sandwiches from a very pale yellow (quinined) member of staff. But, that was my very first teaching experience, and, I thought, well, I quite like this kind of thing.

I wrote to Betty. She wrote to me. Our letters would take four to six weeks to arrive. Perhaps never arrive. Or arrive in the wrong order. But, one kept and re-read all that one had. The worst period was when the bombing started in earnest back home. Knightswood didn't get the full impact of the Clydebank Blitz but had some fringe bombing. Betty and her family were in their Anderson shelter for the two very bad nights. Windows were blown out. The school behind had a direct hit – and a house just further down. Friends took Betty's family over to their house on the south-side for a short stay until the worst mess was cleared up. I got all this detail long after I'd heard of the bombing on the radio. We'd been assured that we'd be "advised of casualties" back home. I didn't see how. My friend Cyril Packham's area of London was taking a lot more. We talked a good deal about it. Didn't help! When Betty's letters came, that did help and though the threat persisted there wasn't anything quite so drastic after that. But, home was more dangerous than active service!

The photographs I have reflect a kind of free, thoughtless life. We lived, day-to-day, that way, reacting to what was in front of us. Our "tropic" was a kind of glass case. We were isolated yet free. In my diary I kept records, just before going home on December 16, 1941.

"The sky, the sea, a young man and a dry pen... the old silence."

Jack Rillie
Glasgow
2003

The Volunteer

Ask me not why, when the cherry bloomed
and the apple flower sickened in life's orchard,
in the year's maytime I chose these emblems
and sat by the saffroned rivers and wept.

The common comforts of the hearth, the white
ecstasies of bright hair and young-limbed loveliness
withheld not their peculiar magnetisms
swinging resolve from the hour's true north.

There was death in the apple, green death
for the bite of the milk teeth, a tang keen
on the soft red gums. The tree was heavy
with unseasonable fruit and the hard boughs
bristled with knives. It is certain only
that no empurpled ikon panoplied
with deceiving vestments drew my fealty
to its canting sacraments. My blood
slewed towards a more rich content than death
ennobled, harboured in its secret tides
the narwhal and the shell with oceans in its throat,
love's gold oysters ripe with ungathered pearls.

Ask me not why I chose a coward's misery
: – a hero's death. There are my bloody hands,
there is my sin and the sin of my kind. Kneeling
I live my Gethsemane but where is my Cross?

No. 7357274's Apologia

My mind was tuned
and keyed with nervous fingers
to a rebel hate
of crashing war.
I smelled its stench
in the songs
of dead singers.
I knew its traitor-issue,
its addled egg.
I was forewarned
in clamant pamphlet,
satire, poem and story
of the wanton invitation
of fife and drum and flag.
I boasted my penetration
and discerned the shadow
of a Flander's Cross
in every flapping banner,
the siren beckon
in politician's braggadocio.
I loved the hearth fires
of peace, the carpet-comfort
and the silent service
of books. The teas
tinkling and sparkling
with talk
in golden afternoons.
Love in the purple bloom
of summer twilights
and in long nights
of fireglow.
These only,
all these
were my possessions.
This was the nest
in the budded

hedgerow I knew
the blunt hands
of war would harry.
My bitterness
was voluble in
cloister, quad and lounge.
I gospelled at
the coffee table's
tête-à-tête and etched
the war monger's
diabolism
with corrosive wrath.
This I averred
and that vehemently
affirmed.
But Hate
burning in the brain
pulsing venom
thru the parts
I never felt
until I saw
a child's plump
fending arm,
its sky-averted eyes.
Grey street
sprouting flame
and a broken body
reddening the cobbles
with its 10-years life.
Then
I knew no shame
of khaki
no stigma
of life-betrayal
in the robes
of nemesis.

I

To Foreign Fields
August 1940

The country from which Jack was departing was in a most fragile and perilous state. Nearly a year had passed since Britain had declared war on a rampant Nazi Germany, and in that time there was little cheer for Britain or its Allies. On June 22, 1940, France had formally submitted to the emboldened German leader Adolf Hitler – who compounded French humiliation when he made them sign the terms of surrender in the same railway carriage where Germany had itself officially surrendered in 1918 – just weeks after Allied troops had bid a hasty retreat from an advancing German army to the beaches of Dunkirk, a French port on the English Channel. Yet, it was between the end of May and the beginning of June 1940, that the name Dunkirk was to be indelibly emblazoned onto the minds of Britons everywhere as a military defeat turned propaganda victory.

The British Expeditionary Force (BEF), sent to defend Belgium against the Nazi onslaught, had found itself increasingly outmanoeuvred and outmuscled by a rampaging German war machine, which, having begun its campaign against western Europe on May 10, 1940, with air raids on Belgium and Holland, followed by parachute drops and rapid land attacks, was ruthlessly unleashing its devastating military technique of combined arms warfare. Together with its French and Belgian allies, the BEF found they were no match for Germany's "Blitzkrieg" – or lightning war – and thousands of troops fell back on Dunkirk, northern France. Between May 26 and June 4, 220 naval vessels, joined by everything from lifeboats and paddle steamers to fishing boats and motor boats, ran the gauntlet of the English Channel in Operation Dynamo, which succeeded in lifting some 338,000 Allied troops from the purgatory-like swell of Dunkirk and into the comparative safety of mainland Britain. Winston Churchill, who had only been prime minister since early May, called it "a miracle of deliverance". And, as Britain lived to fight another day, so it proved.

Soon afterwards, and briefly mentioned in Jack's own introduction, were the spirited and now legendary aerial dogfights between the Royal Air

Force (RAF) and the German Luftwaffe in what was later christened the Battle of Britain. With all France now essentially Nazi conquered territory – the terms of the armistice had left Germany in control over most of the country, including Paris and the entire northern and western reaches – Hitler turned his attentions sharply towards breaking British spirits. With victory over Britain a conceivable aim, Hermann Goering, the head of the Luftwaffe, was instructed to immobilise the RAF's capabilities to such a degree that it could "no longer muster any power of attack worth mentioning against the German crossing".[3]

And, so between early-July and the end of October 1940, the skies above southern England were the scene of some ferocious engagements as German Messerschmitts battled British Hawker Hurricanes and Supermarine Spitfires for complete aerial supremacy. Germany, looking to soften up Britain's defences in preparation for a full-scale invasion, began by attacking shipping in the English Channel and targeting coastal towns, and by August the Luftwaffe had intensified their aerial assaults, focusing on RAF airfield and radar installations. By the end of the first week in August, close to 100 British fighter-jets had been lost as opposed to 190-plus German aircraft.

It was against this tumultuous backdrop that Jack reluctantly took leave from the land of his birth, away from the comforting presence of his parents and the all-consuming love of his new wife, and towards a vast expanse of ocean, wild uncertainty – of his destination, of when he would return, of whether he would return at all – ringing in his ears.

"I was stricken dumb in all my senses by the magnitude of the loss before me," he poignantly notes.

Diary

For Betty –
semper amabo
    dulce ridentem
        dulce loquentem
            uxorem

Commenced 7th September 1940.
Retrospectively from 5th August 1940.

5th August 1940

Perhaps it was nothing more than wishful thinking but until today I had no dread of this eventuality. I envisaged the possibility, but as nothing more than an hypothesis. I was deliciously in love with my wife. The war seemed only an irksome interval breaking the continuity of our love and our life, but only for a little. But to leave Britain and home for heaven knows how many YEARS! Why, it was too unutterably tragic to contemplate. It simply wasn't in the nature of things for it to be true.

> I consequently left Clevedon in a state bordering on dream. And this feeling persisted long after we had left the shores of Scotland.

I consequently left Clevedon in a state bordering on dream. And this feeling persisted long after we had left the shores of Scotland.

There was the usual wearisome and unnecessarily protracted parade before the orderly room in Hallam Road. Then the toiling backbreaking march under a burning sun to the station. Full marching order, kit-bags under the left arm! Capt. Montgomery striding out in front, sergeants barking the step at our heels, 'Eft', 'ight', 'Eft', 'ight', like angry curs; the men, a cursing, sweating rabble trailing their kits along the ground, shifting them from shoulder to shoulder; barging into one another, someone's battle-bowler knocked off, rolling with a clatter into the gutter, the owner cursing, "Bugger it", and leaving it to lie there.

Another delay at the station. We all unhitched our harness and squatted, swilling parched throats with water, sending kids for lemonade. There were women at the railings, staring curiously, and wives and sweethearts and casual lovers strung along the long untidy ranks; the casuals' gay and high pitched chatter cut in on the silence of the men's wives who were there, fear in their hearts, tears in their eyes. In the midst of all this leave-taking, I was alone and it was better so. Betty was already far away. It mattered little to me where I went or when. There was none of the conclusiveness or finality of goodbyes on leaving Clevedon, and I was thus able to slur over the acute reality of it. As I said: it was half a dream. Presently I should wake.

The train arrived and we shuffled and bundled ourselves into the carriages, keeping together as far as possible our own little cliques. Then the familiar palaver of trains about to leave stations. Banging of carriage doors, an agitated feminine voice gasping if this was the train for so and so, and the porter's answer drowned in the Sgt. Major's voice whipping up some stragglers, "Get a move on there". Whistle cuts a pause in the last hurried goodbyes, the taut little arpeggio flutters of a white handkerchief on the drab platform, and the train pulls out in spasmodic movements, becoming smoother as speed increases.

We settle back, open our blouses and the top buttons of our trousers. Cigarettes go round and soon the air is dense with tobacco fumes. Conversation is sparse, someone jerks out a conventional comment, another nods, adds yes, and repeats it. There is nothing to say but silly conventional things, but anything is better than silence. I am still trying to think about home as if I were leaving it behind, but still I cannot believe it. Saddler is strumming his banjo on two notes somewhere down the train, and there are voices singing, "When I'm cleanin' windows", the flood of the cheap, jigging little tune giving the banjo the deceptive sound of beating out the melody. Levy jerks his head significantly, "Christ, I wish he'd learn to play". We nod.

The train spins thru the squalid warehouses and smoke blackened slums of Bristol; Newport with its low mean brick dwellings and the Channel shining in the distance. At Pontypool, tea and a thick sandwich of Bully beef. Shadows lengthen over the countryside and we slip into a waking sleep. Adams starts humming a hymn. I join in softly, sleepily. The sentimental nostalgia of the tune somehow fits our mood, like a lament; and we sort of laze mentally in the ooze of self-pity. Now, there is only intermittent sleep in the dark compartment, the hot fetid stench of cramped, heavily-clothed bodies and the odour of stale tobacco. Someone snores in the next compartment, and over in the corner of ours Arnott gets a boot in his ear and curses in his unintelligible south-country dialect. Feeling restless, I imagine, Adams attempts conversation. "I wonder where we are?" and "Near Crewe I should think". A desultory dialogue ensues. I suddenly think of a way by which we could have dodged this journey. It seems foolproof we agree and we curse ourselves for not having thought of it before. But I think we both knew we really would never have attempted the scheme, audacious tho it was. The practise of formulating such schemes is only an attempt to combat the feeling of impotence which Army handling breeds in one. Shrewsbury, Crewe. On northwards.

6th August 1940

The train snakes thru sleeping towns, thru the scraggy dark Midland counties. Dawn breaks cold and grey south of Carlisle. Scotland and the green familiar slopes of the Southern Uplands, a wispy scarf of mist thrown round their peaks. Beattock Summit and a remembrance of Cunninghame Graham's short story. It must have been such a day as this he describes. Everyone on edge as we near Glasgow, jokes from Scotsmen about jumping out. We cross the Clyde Bridge and have a brief glimpse of buses and one of the "new-cars" which we Glaswegians are so proud of. Pedestrians look up casually at the bridge, but they don't see us, they don't know we are going out to some disease-ridden colony, and even if they did they wouldn't care. I think of Betty and the six bus and the clanging of the little green gate behind me. The carriage door is not locked. No one would see me slip out.

Why not? Why? The answer has been haunting me since war started. It is because I'm afraid, afraid of military prison, of disgrace after the war? Yet I have no sympathy with the war; I should hold myself morally blameless if I deserted; but the spectre might rise again in post-war life and blight not my life only, but Betty's also. I hate the army. I hate the war. They're all wrong, they're criminal. I must swallow my hatred – meanwhile – for the sake of our happiness. It is worth it. Perhaps in the last resort the war too is worth it...

So the flux and reflux of self-recrimination and self-approval goes on. This tumultuous, shifting mire of thought ebbs and flows. But I am not feeling, neither tears are there nor any emotion at all. Only deep down a dull heavy ache, as tho my emotions had been drugged. I was leaving Betty, I was near her but not a tear rose to my eye. Then there came to me a conviction that Wordsworth's "thoughts that do often lie too deep for tears" was authentic. I was stricken dumb in all my senses by the magnitude of the loss before me.

The train moved off and ran down the silver streak of the Clyde to Gourock. There was Kilcreggan and Cove opposite, the white houses glistening in a shaft of sunlight streaming thru a rift in the clouds. And I took Adams and Packham to the end of the pier and pointed out Kirn, the red domes of its pier superstructure shining dimly thru the mist of rain. The great peaks behind the Holy Loch jostling each other in the purple gloom, which clothes them on even the most brilliant days.

We sat on the quayside and a seagull shit on Levy's helmet, much to his disgust. Mugs of steaming hot tea, bully beef and potatoes in their jackets appeared miraculously. We were not hungry but we contrived to tuck the lot away and batten it down with a thick slice of bread and margarine.

The long wait for the tender was fraying our ragged nerves. Packham was a bit white. Someone crudely blamed it on the last three nights he had spent with his wife. No one laughed. Levy admitted he was feeling a bit queer round his viscera and, "I don't mind where we're going but I don't fancy this sea-voyage". He voiced everyone's feelings and we were all relieved and considerably brighter for a time.

Queen Mary II took us on board the H.M.S. Canton. It seemed huge, towering far above us, sailors just specks as they hung over the rail. Assembly on the quarterdeck. We were shown to our sleeping quarters and mess and then left alone.

The mattresses are musty and thin, made of sacking. L., P., and I snoop around, collar three blue flock ones, soft and comfortable. Some other unfortunates get ours.

We scarcely noticed the movement of the ship as we weighed anchor and nosed our way down the estuary. But someone had noticed and ran to tell us. We all rushed upstairs and on the port side Kirn slid past. I could see Argyll Terrace quite plainly, the little nook where Betty and I sat in the sun, the Queen's Hotel, the woods above the golf course. I picked them all out eagerly to Adams. Maybe he was bored; enthusiasm, which one does not share, is prone to becoming intensely boring. But he had the good sense to say nothing, to let me talk. I did; and then felt suddenly shy and shut up.

> We passed Dunoon, hearing the Tower clock sprinkle its chimes over the still waters. 6 o'clock. The Cloch not yet lit. Wemyss Bay with memories of primroses in the wood. Largs with snug little Millport on the To port. Ailsa Craig & the hazy, jagged peaks of Arran.

We passed Dunoon, hearing the Tower clock sprinkle its chimes over the still waters. 6 o'clock. The Cloch not yet lit. Wemyss Bay with memories of primroses in the wood. Largs with snug little Millport to port. Ailsa Craig and the hazy, jagged peaks of Arran.

Just here a reconnaissance plane picked us up, circling us and signalling in Morse. "Danger. Submarines". We

H.M.S. Canton

altered our course imperceptibly and when eventually we noticed the Craig again on our port bow our hearts beat wildly. Were we turning back to Gourock? Had the trip been cancelled? Home? And for a moment we actually believed ourselves homeward bound again. Then a sailor decoded for us the plane's message and before he had finished talking the plane itself had returned, with its light twinkling and winking wisely. It circled three times, then headed for the coast. "All clear, Canton. Goodnight and good luck". It was our last link with Britain. It was gone.

A soft rain wrapped us round; it was chilly, and we went below as the Mull faded into the mist.

We had a supper of fish and chips, both of which tasted strange. After supper we talked for a bit, agreed morosely that there was no turning back now. Rumours were circulating thick and fast and we believed or rejected them according to our whim.

Packham suggested a stroll on deck. There were no stars and it had grown colder. We chatted for a bit to the "standby" on the gun and heard for the first time our destination. He was an Aberdonian and in the broad lilting Highland dialect he gave us to understand that Hell was a pleasure resort in comparison with Sierra Leone. As decently as we could we fled from the dismal lugubrious tale and went below. Later we discussed the prospect and deciding that there could be no need for us in Freetown, we came to the glib conclusion that we should be transferred to another ship and taken elsewhere. The topic was being argued and reviewed by little subdued knots of men in odd corners of the ship. Everyone had a plausible explanation of why we were not staying there, too plausible. We all knew and were shocked. Sierra Leone was our destination.

For a little the vibration and the slight pitch of the ship made sleep impossible, then gently, imperceptibly we sank into a deep easeful drowse. The blankets were soft and warm; the motion of the ship was pleasant, dreamy; outside the hush–HUSH of the waves. Dropping, dropping, down into the warmth, the oblivion of sleep, deep, dreamless.

7th August 1940

I felt amazingly refreshed when I awoke and a little surprised to discover that we had not been threatened or sunk by U-boats. Life-boat drill. Montgomery decided that we should set a watch. When we were allotted to our stations we discovered that in each case we were covered by a navy-man. The position was ridiculous; we were so obviously superfluous. It satisfied the man no doubt to see us occupied and accorded with his childish, petty notions of soldiering.

He began publishing orders, bulging with, "Thou shalt nots". We were privileged with certain decks to ourselves (those congested with tackle and winding gear) and graciously given permission to use the windy side of the promenade and upper decks. In short, everything was done to prevent the officer's eyes being encumbered with the sight of us.

7th August 1940

I felt amazingly refreshed when I awoke & a little surprised to discover that we had not been threatened or sunk by U-boats. Life-boat drill. Montgomery decided that we should set a watch. When we were allotted to our stations we discovered that in each case we were covered by a navy-man. The position was ridiculous; we were so obviously superfluous. It satisfied the man no doubt to see us occupied & accorded with his childish, petty notions of soldiering.

So the ship ploughed on. The 8th of August, the 9th, 10th, 11th passed with grey skies and heavy seas. Many were sick, in particular a man by the name of Strangeways. He was an odd scrawny little fellow, with a long pinched face, a thin hawk nose and close-set eyes. His complexion was positively green with sickness and his face more thin and wedge shaped than ever. Levy and I met him strolling up the deck one forenoon, unearthly pale but apparently merely taking some air. Suddenly he shot over to the rail, vomited casually overboard and continued unconcernedly on his way. It was done with as little fuss as expectoration and the spectacle was irresistibly ludicrous. He heard the gust of Levy's laughter and turned and shook a knobbly fist at us. "I'll do for you, Levy," he shouted, and the thought of him "doing for" anyone at that moment absolutely convulsed us. Packham retold the story, with histrionics, in the mess and everyone screamed.

It is a strange world, that of a ship at sea. As tho part of the earth had detached itself and was meandering with its cargo of humanity thru uncharted space. The movement of life is arrested. Men go thru the motions of living but they are cut adrift from their roots. Here there is neither birth, nor copulation, nor death, only life jerking rather uncertainly between the barren sea and the leaden sky.

> There is no change from day to day
> I still feel I might just be anchored off
> The Scottish coast, with land & home just
> over the horizon.

There is no change from day to day and I still feel I might just be anchored off the Scottish coast, with land and home just over the horizon.

I have been thinking of Betty a great deal those last few days. Realising how dependant I was on her love, reliving often our honeymoon, planning the future that could never be certain amid the constant dangers of the sea. I feel calmer now, settled down to a steadier, more mature love. It has become the background of all my life, unchanging, colouring all my thoughts and actions, a part of my being. As for Betty, I might just be visiting her this afternoon, or perhaps have just left her. It is a very real, comfortable, satisfying kind of love. And in a wistful kind of way I am fairly happy.

Somewhere about 12th August we made our first encounter with shipping. A cruiser appeared on the horizon and in a trice our guns were weaving for her range. She challenged us. And again, minatorily, "You are slow in replying". We answered hastily. She was British – thank heaven – and with a brusque, "Very good", she passed on her way.

The sun was warmer now, the days clear and cloudless, the nights hung thick with stars.

I read somewhat desultorily several novels among them Talbot Mundy's "Caesar Dies". A bit lush in parts and fails slightly in a half-hearted and spasmodic attempt to reproduce Latin syntax and manner. Still it gives a full and accurate picture of the half-mad, sadistic successor of Aurelius and the maze of intrigue and corruption, which enmeshed Rome in the beginning of her decadence.

Saroyan's famous "Daring Young Man" pleased me immensely and I read and re-read the stories until I was saturated with the technique that seems to make you an eavesdropper on his mental processes. I wrote a short story of my own and found the trick not supremely difficult to master.

The story and four letters I wrote were the only positive brainwork I did in all the 10-days at sea. Mainly we idled and talked and slept in the hot afternoons.

On 14th August the buzzer sounded for action stations. As we ran with helmet and emergency rations to our cover we saw the grey plume of smoke on the horizon, which marked our quarry. We were battened down and compelled to wait the outcome in ignorance. Outside the clatter of bells and the voices of the gun-crew as they called out the range, and thru the clamour the rattle and screech of the davits as the cutter was prepared to take off the boarding party. For 90 minutes we lay in the half-gloom, our fear and its sequel of excitement had faded and we were nearly all half asleep. I had my head on my helmet, and was curled round a pillar, dead to the world, when the rattle of bolts woke me and we shuffled out, blinking in the strong sunlight. The provoker of all the commotion was pitching in our wash about 100 yds astern – a Spanish collier!

Early on the morning of 16th August we had our first glimpse of the African coast, a long grey line on our starboard bow. We were pre-occupied most of the morning with the business of packing. About 10.00 hrs we slid into Freetown harbour and stood to attention on the quarterdeck as the ship dropped anchor.

The harbour was crammed with shipping, naval vessels of all descriptions, at least six liners bulging with troops, oil tankers, cargo boats and a varied assortment of lighters and barges.

We had lunch then waited around in groups to go ashore. As time went on and there was no hint of disembarking the rumour sprang up that we were going aboard another troop ship. It became lavishly embroidered and it was said we were bound for Somaliland or Shanghai. The sergeant who confirmed the rumour of our transfer to the Monarch of Bermuda, scotched the others. There was no accommodation for us ashore, neither nets nor beds, our supply ship having been sunk a week previous to our arrival.

> At 16.00 hours the tender drew alongside & we left the Canton.

At 16.00 hours the tender drew alongside and we left the Canton.

H.M.S. Canton was a P&O pleasure liner of 16,000 tons converted into an armed cruiser. Her armament consisted of eight 6-inch guns and two A.A. guns. The decks had been reinforced to carry the guns but she had not been otherwise re-fitted. The exquisite woodwork had been preserved and the swimming pool and cinema were still in operation (we had two talkie shows during the voyage).

I was particularly struck with the efficiency of the Navy. The men go about their jobs without fuss or interference from their superiors. They dress anyhow while on duty and it was quite a common sight to see them going around in sweater and flannels. The main object was the job in hand. In the Army the emphasis is entirely misplaced. Men are almost universally ignorant of the duties for which they are mustered while in the art of spit and polish they are more than proficient. The result is a glittering facade, which conceals behind it an appalling tangle of inefficiency, discontent and ignorance. The Navy inspires confidence; the Army begs for it. To anyone who knows the Army, the series of "strategic withdrawals" with which it has distinguished itself is by no means a matter for surprise. Incompetence so blatantly obvious in the ranks must necessarily extend to our General Staff with whom rests the organisation and tactics involved in all military operations. Our Army's training is pitifully inadequate and the staff work is uninformed, pedestrian and completely lacking in foresight and initiative. Our Navy is more than pulling its weight; the work of the R.A.F. is incomparably brilliant. On these two forces depend victory. The Army has become the "Sick Man of the Forces".

The Monarch of Bermuda was anchored not 200 yds from the Canton. The tender steamed slowly up to her, circled, and made off back to the Canton. She had forgotten a barge. It took some considerable time to tie up that barge to the vessel's side but ultimately it was done and we set off again. The going this time was painfully slow and to make things more difficult a heavy sea was rising. When at length we reached hailing distance the pilot decided to take the ship on our other side, i.e. to sandwich the barge between ourselves and the "Monarch". It was growing dark, 100 men were

Monarch of Bermuda

standing jammed on the narrow deck of the tender, equipped with full pack. Our shoulders were aching, our legs were tired and it was stiflingly hot. But we began to sing, old sentimental tunes, popular music-hall choruses, ribald army rags. It was now 18.00 hrs; we had taken two hours to cover 200 yds!! And still we weren't on board. It was dark. We were hungry and fed-up. Twice the mooring ropes slipped, then one snapped and the frayed end sang thru the air above our heads with the speed of a whiplash. More manoeuvring for position. The barge was about 20 feet below the hatchway and a rope ladder was lowered to allow us to board. The men crossed the deep sucking gap between the tender and the barge and awaited their turn on the heaving, sloping deck. Twice again the moorings slipped as men were reaching for the swaying ladder, and they were almost tossed down into the seething fury between the barge and ship's side. At last my own turn. Jump from tender to barge, deck rising to meet my feet, landing on all fours, scrambling for a handhold and finding none, someone grabbing me by the shoulders. Ok. Deck steadier now. Filing towards ladder. Barge dashing side, breaking away. Wild grab for rungs. Got it. Kit sagging on my shoulders pulling me back, arms trembling with the strain. Up, up, up. The little square of light growing. At last, safe. I look back. A little white-faced Cockney on the end of the swaying, twisting ladder. Scared, an acrophobic. Poor little beggar. His hand slips, there is a shout of alarm from below. But he's alright, he's making it. I give him my hand, a sailor grabs his collar. We pull him in, trembling all over. "Thanks chum," and he rushes off. I think he's gone to cry. Nervous reaction sort of thing.

So it went on.

It was 20.00 hrs before everyone was safely aboard! Grudgingly the steward was persuaded to give us supper. Bread & cheese & we were still hungry. They said it was a "dead loss to the ship."!!

It was 20.00 hrs before everyone was safely aboard! Grudgingly the steward was persuaded to give us supper. Bread and cheese and we were still hungry. They said it was a "dead loss to the ship"!!

We slept that night on mattresses on the floor of the great dance hall. The following day we had a chance to look round the giant luxury liner. Every inch of her spelt affluence. She was built to cater in every detail for the pampered tastes of Hollywood stars and the myriads of idle socialites who leave New York for the playground of Bermuda. The food we were served with was execrable, often completely uneatable. To make our lot harder we had the ridiculous contrast of the Officers' Mess where French windows opened directly onto our sleeping quarters. They were supplied with eight meals per day. The food was as varied as that of the best hotels and the service equalled it. We returned from emptying a nauseating meal in the swill-tub and sat and watched hungrily the high-class food, which passed thru on trolleys to the Officers' Mess.

The heat was suffocating. The water was turned off from 8.00 hrs each morning and we had nothing to drink all day. We were almost crazy with thirst, but tho the officers had crate upon crate of beer, minerals and iced water we could get nothing. We complained. "The officers understand but they can do nothing. They're sorry". The canteen said no beer, refused to get any. No biscuits to buy, no chocolate, nothing.

Thirst, bad food. Our letters home full of our sufferings. Censored... Heat, sweat, sleeplessness, thirst, hunger. We were desperate, but helpless.

Te Vermiculum Laudamus [4]

Observe.
Blind in the earth the worm
in the root-jungle wandering eyeless.
To the starless night
no dawns bring grey disillusion,
no twilights deceive
in the world-without-end darkness
in the subsoil night
no striving in this world
of no horizons. No rainbow-gold,
no fearful tomorrows and no
regretful yesterdays there
in that sunlessness.
But only the dawdling
serpentine progress from
blackness to darkness
there
in the earth's labyrinths.
Compare.
The sightless mind,
past-burdened,
tunnelling dreadfully
from the grave of now
into the lightlessness
of a tomorrow's tomb.

The Poor

You cannot count the eyes
You need not know the names
You cannot interpret the words.
They are myriad
They are without significance
They are babel.

And the eyes of the poor are quick
With painful mysteries
And the names of the poor are holy
As the sons of God's
And the words of the poor are fresh
As God's wounds.

You can see them if you care
In the streets far from suburbs
Or folded between commerce
And the river's edge,
Or you may go unafraid
To the cul-de-sac
Where they dwell.

Brightness visits here briefly
Staying on walls.
Like leper-skin lit by a dream
Of impossible hereafters.

And death. O
Fold the rough hands,
Turn the clean face
To the wall. Eternity stands
By the area railings.

There is so much ripeness
There is so much simplicity
There is so little fulfilment
And it is too easy to be just

In the terms of your indictment.
It is perhaps harder to remember
Gay weeds clinging to brickwork
And the yearling's first essay
At speech adding a moiety
Of pride to three generations.
It is easy to forget
The faces that bloom at windows
On Sunday mornings
Observing without emotion
Anabasis of churchgoers
And the mad career of a tramcar
In the empty street
Like a Saturday drunk.
It is difficult to recall also
The hectic voices of children
Flaring in the dusk.

There on the threshold
Between dusk and dark
Between Calvary and Calton
Is the same barter
Of small cares and satisfactions
Annihilating the reality.

Break bread and be wise
Remembering the broken body
Of the living
And the long redemption aeon
Of the grand and terrible poor.

II

No Place Like Freetown
August 1940 to October 1940

As Jack tried to come to terms with his first experience of active service, bad weather back home had given pilots on both sides of the British-German divide some much needed rest as the Battle of Britain took a few days hiatus in mid-August. But, the aerial cat and mouse games soon began again, and the last two weeks of the month saw both the RAF and Luftwaffe sustain heavy losses. German aircraft were falling out of the skies above England at a far greater rate, however, and by the end of August the Luftwaffe had lost an excess of 600 planes compared to just about half that number for the RAF.

The wilds of Freetown and Sierra Leone were, in the meantime, presenting Jack with other challenges. As he surveyed his surroundings, and the stark reality of life in the tropics hit him with his first intake of breath, he was unafraid to take on everything from the "lot of the native" to the "hopelessly incompetent" drill instructors. Freetown's City Hotel was also the subject of Jack's ire early on, due to its requisitioning by British officers, and while he makes only a passing reference to the hotel in his war diary, the City became a legend in its own right thanks to the work of Graham Greene. In his work of fiction, The Heart of the Matter, *the one-time literary editor and film critic of* The Spectator *wrote of the City Hotel – under the assumed name of the Bedford – and in his 1936 travel book,* Journey Without Maps, *he made direct references to the hotel itself as he plotted his trip to the sinister unknowns of Liberia. This passage from Greene's travelogue, written just several years before Jack himself set foot in the Sierra Leone capital, provides an intriguing – if quirky – snapshot of life in pre-war Freetown.*

"I wanted to do a pub crawl. But one can't crawl very far in Freetown. All one can do is to have a drink at the Grand and then go and have a drink at the City. The City is usually more crowded and noisy because there's a billiard table; people are rather more dashing, get a little drunk and tell indecent stories; but not if there's a woman present. I had never found

myself in a place which was more protective to women... These men in the City bar, prospectors, shipping agents, merchants, engineers, had to reproduce English conditions if they were to be happy at all."[5]

Greene wasn't so taken with this "English capital city"[6] – "Nature... *rising in tree-covered hills above the sea and the town, a dull uninteresting green, was powerless to carry off the shabby town"*[7] – and neither was Jack. Where the English-born author – then in his thirties, and having never previously ventured beyond Europe prior to his West African odyssey – thought *"everything ugly in Freetown was European"*[8] and *"anything beautiful in the place... was native"*[9], Jack – having never before even left the shores of Great Britain prior to the war, and from his vantage point of the military hospital on Mount Aureol hundreds of feet above sea-level – thought its *"indisputable... beauty"* of the *"evil, deceptive kind"*.

By September, and as the Battle of Britain saw Churchill attack some of Germany's industrial centres and Hitler the likes of London and its docks, the so-called "Dakar affair" was another one of the many competing items of news dominating Jack's penned accounts of war on the west coast of Africa. Between September 23 and 25, 1940, the Senegalese capital was the scene of a daring military bid to land British and Free French troops in an attempt to capture this port city lest it be used by the Vichy French West African regime of governor-general Pierre Boisson as a base for German U-boats and surface raiders. But, the attack, code-named Operation Menace, ended in failure for the Allies as the large British naval deployment, which included the British battleship, HMS Resolution, was robustly matched by the local French forces in Dakar, who, contrary to hopes, failed to rally to the cause of Free French leader, Charles de Gaulle, and instead remained loyal to Pétain's Vichy government based in the unoccupied zone of France. The British and Free French raiding party, in what was one of the sorrier episodes of the Allied war effort, was forced to abandon its plans for an ambitious takeover of this piece of French West Africa and de Gaulle was left humiliated.

"The whole affair depressed me tremendously," records Jack.

Diary

27th August 1940

When they called for an advance party I was only too ready to volunteer. The tender took an Essex, RASC and an F.A advance party besides ourselves. Although we were all bound for different billets the kits were slumped together in one huge inconglomerate heap. Unloading was therefore unnecessarily difficult and protracted. Eight of our kit-bags were lost in transit, two of them being mine. And so half-hearted were the efforts made to find them that for three weeks I owned only the clothes I stood up in, which, in this climate where they must be changed every day, was almost unbearable. However, I borrowed a P.T. kit from Packham and strolled round in that while my clothes were washed and dried.

> We had our first experience of mosquito nets. the night we landed y found them no deterrent to sleep. But they did look rather amusing at first – like a string of dumplings hanging from the rafters.

We had our first experience of mosquito nets the night we landed and found them no deterrent to sleep. But they did look rather amusing at first – like a string of dumplings hanging from the rafters.

We were billeted in the old hospital, a solid two-storey building of whitewashed stone. Like all the houses of the colony it had verandas all round and broad overhanging eaves. Inside it was cool and clean in the long white wards. The shutters were of Venetian type and the windows

Jack, extreme right, walking with two colleagues

opened inwards, allowing therefore the maximum ventilation. We were mercifully equipped too with sprays and baths, tho cold.

For those four days on the advance party we worked 10 hours every day, stripped to the waist and streaming in sweat. Thirty tons of equipment we took from the docks and stored away. There were a dozen or so black dock labourers to help us but we found them incorrigibly slow. Still, the pittance which they were given (1/- per day) did not justify hashing. 1/- per day and they were almost all married!! The cost of living in Freetown is obstreperously high and how they contrived to subsist themselves far less keep a family on 6/- a week I can't imagine. The lot of the native is notoriously hard.

The inhabitants of the Colony are a mixed bag of various tribes amongst which the Krus and the Mendes preponderate. They have that charming and disturbing mixture of naiveté and cunning which is common to all such tribes. They are cheerful and lazy, loyal and friendly people. The existence of Irish names amongst their families is due to the invasion and intermarriage of a number of Irish pirates in an earlier century.

The lure of Western custom proved too strong for them and leaving a life which tho primitive was natural and dignified they flocked to do the bidding of the white man. Decorating themselves with the fripperies of Europeanism they neglected the realities. They clung to their superstitions while they seized the adornments of English clothes. They are for the most part unskilled, and cut adrift from their familiar apparatus of living and working they gravitate inevitably towards casual, ill paid, menial employment. They live and breed prolifically in squalid ill-ventilated hovels built of corrugated iron sheets. They are governed under the "democratic" principles, which Britain so magnanimously bequeaths on her colonies. But they have not the sense of equality, which is one of its postulates. In every way financially, mentally, morally, physically they are made to feel their inferiority to the whites and the complex has become so deeply seated that they accept their position as freed slaves. Our boys work for 12 men for £1 per month. If they ask for more they are promptly sacked and others engaged. Labour is cheap and abundant. Wherein does their freedom consist? (Perhaps in the choice of death and semi-starvation). In many ways their condition is disturbingly analogous to that of the freed slaves in the decadent days of Rome.

The veneer of civilisation lies on their lives like an ugly stain. The black in Africa is a terribly, pitifully, tragic figure. His problem is difficult but not by any means insoluble. When "The wheel is come full circle"[10]...

30th August 1940

The main party landed. It is 14 days since we left the Canton, 25 days since leaving England. It was glaringly obvious in the weeks which were to follow how inadequate were the arrangements made for our arrival. The War Office must have known of our destination weeks before we left, yet they could only spare us 48 hours leave; tho we lay out in Freetown harbour for 14 days and when we did land the billets were still in a shocking state of unpreparedness.

The main body were quartered in the new wooden shacks at the top of the hill. Sanitation was non-existent. Everyone had diarrhoea from the food eaten on the Bermuda and for the first few days it was a common sight to see rows of squatting figures on the edge of the jungle, joking about it in the daytime, at night cursing.

Two-thousand troops landed on that day and found that there were no adequate rations for that number, and furthermore, that the increase would not be forthcoming for at least 10 days. Our meals were meagre, badly cooked and of low quality. Nor were there any eating-houses of any kind at that time in Freetown, the officers having appropriated The City Hotel for their own use. There was a good deal of grousing and bickering which only needed slight provocation before swelling into open revolt. But our grievances were mollified by the excuses

A Freetown cooking scene

Jack, Freetown

and sympathy and promises of the Q.M. who assured us that the officers were suffering the same privations. We knew this latter to be a lie, but resolved to wait and see if things would improve.

Adams was billeted in these huts and I did not see much of him during the following few days. I missed him a bit I must confess, for tho the high spirited, alert minded Packham and the shrewd Levy are admirable friends, few people I have ever met can claim the knack of harmonising with another person's moods as Adams does. When I am gay, Willie is too; when I grow morose he is likewise. Willie never irritates by imposing a contrasting mood on yours. Yet he possesses an amazingly strong character and no one will ever budge him from his principles. He and I agreed one day in deploring the mercenary spirit, which pervaded the legal profession. He confessed it was a profession entirely without moral scruples and reiterated the vow that I had heard from him before that it was his duty and the duty of all young men to clear the corruption from the system and set it on a true professional basis. He had read Wells on this subject and agreed that the professions ought to be actuated by the desire to serve the community and by the love of so doing. He insists on that principle and follows it sincerely.

Some days later he came down to the old building, however, and the four of us were united again.

We were in the middle of the rainy season and the days followed each other in blazing forenoons and torrential downpours. The night sky emblazoned with stars or lit with the flashes of lightning.

There was nothing for us to do except two hours drill in the early morning. The instructors were hopelessly incompetent, the ground was uneven, the sun hot and the whole business of drill so manifestly pointless. We were a slovenly, dull crew; we knew it and did not care. The N.C.Os threatened and blustered, wheedled and cajoled but to no purpose. I felt acutely the ridiculousness of the spectacle. Thirty men walking in a field. Thirty men turning and stopping and marching again; no destination, no purpose, not even amusing other people by our circus. Sweating, dejected, careless and ludicrous. And the news

A picture of Betty from inside Jack's diary

drifts from our radios of our homes being bombed, our people mangled, maimed, killed. Thirty men under the burning sun tramp the hot red earth, back and forth, without purpose, without destination. There was no answer to our questions. There could be none.

We practised a ceremonial parade for two hours one day and saw the incompetence of our officers too but we did not care. Later the G.O.C. came to see us do it and made a pretty speech. He tells us we are guarding the trade routes of England, and asks us not to mention how uncomfortable we are, how useless we are, and how scurrilously we are being treated – tho not in so many words.

We read voraciously in these days, and discussed our books and our hardships in the evenings. Packham's politics are a deep shade of pink. If we are all possessed of the same energy and bitterness as he after the war we will have a new country and a new government. God give us young Britons the power to hate. Not German injustice and cruelty and inequality only must we hate but British injustice, British cruelty, British inequality. They promise us again as they promised our fathers a world fit for heroes. We must ourselves accomplish the fulfilment of that promise. And whether we win or lose we can do it.

Can Germany take from us the things, which we cherish most? Can it take my wife, my home, my parents? Will it starve me, prevent me from assembling some comforts round me, steal my amusement and my leisure? It can. But it can also take away our rulers' money. I wonder if that is the real thing we are fighting for? For us our homes are the reality. These are our citadels.

I thought much of Betty. And when I got her letters I was in a kind of warm, squelchy paradise. How intensely she lives. Every detail goes down in her letters and fills out her life so accurately I can believe I am there with her again. How I long for her out here! Not only for the love which she gave so tremendously, so freely, but for the way she drew me into life. Betty exerted more on me than her undoubted appeal to my senses. There was something quickly sympathetic about her nature and a strong streak of commonsense. She refused to let her life be ruled by what might have been sheer emotion. Then

Looking out over the red roofs of Freetown today

when we found ourselves and thru three wonderful years proved ourselves deeply in love she gave up every atom of her being to our life. I was and am still, I'm afraid, a bit of a dreamer. I was letting life slip by me by studying in the Zoological Garden of books. Slipping along on the fringes of the stream Betty pulled me into the torrent of the current, and when I edged out pulled me back again and by the strength of her love kept me there.

I ought to be able to stand on my own feet but instead I'm stumbling along, blindly like a stricken child with tears in its eyes, groping along till I see your face again and that warm smile. Then I'll lift my head and pull my shoulders back and go out into the sunlight with you, happy, unafraid, alive.

The days drag on; they are without incident.

I am not enamoured of Freetown and its environs. Indisputably it has beauty but of an evil, deceptive kind. It is like a leper clothed in purple and gold. The hospital is 900 feet above sea level and from this height there is an excellent view of the town. The red roofs cluster among the broad leaves of the palms and green spreading foliage of the huge cotton trees; the white of a tarmac street is fringed by the darker green of the mango tree. The colours shimmer and dance in the great cup of the valley like a kaleidoscope of gaily-painted silks. In the emerald crescent arms of the bay, the ships lift and swing to the gentle swell of the tides. A sea, blue as a girl's eyes, reflects the tiny puffball clouds, which chase one another over a sky scarcely more blue. And over all hangs the vulture, a sinister silhouette in the blue, the hieroglyph of death.

But when you descend the narrow, twisting road, which runs like a red raw weal across the face of the slopes to the town, the illusions of beauty are rudely shattered. The fetid miasma of squalid congested human life is at first almost insufferable. The dwellings of the natives are mean, tumbledown hovels, patched and stained. Their interiors are gloomy, ill ventilated and small. Nearly all have a dark, damp little room set aside for the clients of the female occupants. For more than 70% of the natives will put their wives, mothers, sisters at the disposal of the white man. Brothels are numerous and in the street one is continually pestered by young children touting for their sisters or acting as pimps for one of the larger brothels. Ninety-two per cent of the native population has some form of V.D. Everywhere vice, filth, squalor, debauchery.

The shops, open to the street, are stocked with bright cottons and a hundred and one knick-knacks of Manchester origin. The trade is carried on by Syrians, a mixed... race who treat the natives with... contempt...

The whole town is ugly, jerry-built and badly planned. Nothing has been built for permanence and when a structure threatens to disintegrate it is merely patched up. The old justice-house is grey and scabrous and, built in the heavily ornate style of decadent Victorianism, it is ugly and incongruous. The more recent Government House is more strictly utilitarian, constructed on ample lines but its facade with verandas and railings presents an unhappy resemblance to a block of modern slum-clearance tenements.

There are no amusements except those appealing to the lusts and these are utterly repugnant to me. I must talk and read and write. When these fail me I must fall back on my memories and my dreams.

In the weeks that follow our minds are constantly harassed by news of the invasion having started on England. Everyone agrees that any such news will ultimately be good, in that it will be decisive in one way or the other. And we are all utterly fed-up with the war and the conduct of it. We have no guarantee that if we do win our victory will bring any improvement of political conditions or alleviation of social misery. It is a choice between the benign, muddled, laissez-faire administration of a British Government or the harsh, penetrating, jack-boot efficiency of a German controlled government. Of the two the former is preferable but not worth one cubic centimetre of human blood! And unless we leave the Army with a definite policy and a firm resolve to see it thru, we are destined for a repetition of post-1918 conditions. God give us clear heads, wise counsels and unshakeable wills!

Jack, Freetown

7th September 1940

> 7 Sept. 1940 — London is being bombed. The list of casualties is 400 killed, 1400 injured. Nothing but news of our homes being pulped & we out here in safety. The sense of impotence increases; it is almost suffocating. Impotence & isolation. What care we for the safety of this colony of rotten humanity? Is not our place with our families? Did not we join up to defend them?

London is being bombed. The list of casualties is 400 killed, 1400 injured. Nothing but news of our homes being pulped and we out here in safety. The sense of impotence increases; it is almost suffocating. Impotence and isolation. What care we for the safety of this colony of rotten humanity? Is not our place with our families? Did not we join up to defend them?

The conversation is bitter in the barrack rooms. The question is raised again and again, "What are we fighting for?" No one, not even the dimwits, professes to believe it is Freedom or Democracy. What is it then? Victory. Very good. What then? The ex-servicemen neglected, the maimed forgotten, the workless trodden on, parliamentary haggling and bickering, the whole tragic cycle of 1918-40 and another war to kill our youth and blight our happiness at the end of it? H.G.Wells has a solution but its operation depends on us, not on the Government. Have we the means, the will, the power, to take our salvation out of our ruler's hands in this democratic state of ours?

Ordinary men, scores of inoffensive little Canutes, with peace in their hearts talking at the tides...

Rumours thickened about Dakar. It had been taken. It was occupied. German parachute troops had taken it over. Then at last the radio dispelled those rumours.

Jack, Freetown

22nd September 1940

A French flying boat landed here in Freetown about a week previous to the Dakar affair. It carried General de Gaulle and on several occasions we saw him with our G.O.C. Then the radio announced that de Gaulle was at Dakar with F.F. troops. He had gone there in answer to the request of the colonials who had declared in his favour. His landing party of envoys was almost arrested and in their flight to their launch some were killed by machine-gun fire. The shore-batteries and the Richelieu opened fire on the General and his escorting naval force of British ships. They replied and then withdrew. It would have needed a major military operation to have taken Dakar and de Gaulle shrank from spilling French blood.

27th September 1940

Thus ran the account of the British radio. But it seemed to us another major defeat for our Army Council.

1) They admitted they knew of Italian and German infiltration. Enemy officers taking charge of airfields etc. If the intelligence service was doing its work they also knew roughly the strength of the enemy force and enemy hold over the Government.

2) They allowed thru Gibraltar three French warships, which were used to attack them at Dakar.

3) The Independent Company of British troops were equipped and intended for attack, not for occupying a friendly town.

4) The vital importance of Dakar to our trade was heavily stressed before the affair. As a submarine base in enemy hands it was a serious danger (almost an insuperable one) to our trade. As an airbase it could threaten and render useless this important harbour of Freetown where all our convoys collect.

Jack, Freetown

> De Gaulle did not wish to pit Frenchman
> against Frenchman!! Fiddlesticks !
>
> We've been sold a pup again. Norway, Holland
> Belgium, France, Somaliland, Dakar. What a record !
>
> Is our War Council squeamish, or thoroughly
> inept or ARE WE BEING SOLD OUT ??

De Gaulle did not wish to pit Frenchman against Frenchman!! Fiddlesticks!

We've been sold a pup again. Norway, Holland, Belgium, France, Somaliland, Dakar. What a record!

Is our War Council squeamish or thoroughly inept or ARE WE BEING SOLD OUT??

The whole affair depressed me tremendously. On top of this there was no mail for me. And altogether I felt thoroughly downcast for the two following days. Betty was on my mind a great deal and I was worried over reports of Glasgow being bombed. If she should be hurt or even killed... I tried to imagine life without her, but it just didn't work. It was a cryptogram without the key. It was a maze of disconnected and irrelevant details, a story without plot or sequence. Oh God may she be spared. Tho the whole world go up in flames preserve Betty. Without her the world shrivels to a hand's-breadth, it is flat, stale, unprofitable. I simply could not envisage what it would be like to rap on the door of 321 and find no Betty to open the door, no Betty upstairs bathing, no Betty to sit on the arm of my chair and smoke a cigarette before we go out. There can't be a world, which does not contain these things. Somehow I have confidence, or faith, in her safety and the inviolability of our love.

Might it be wishful thinking? Then I wish the consummation into existence.

With the conclusion of the Dakar incidents and the return here of the I.C. and the F.F. troops we had our first raid. I had been chosen to play in a trial game of soccer at King

"Our 'Boy', Tamba (with family), washed, ironed, cleaned and ran errands for three of us daily. An intelligent, willing, religious man with some (church) education. Wrote me a letter after I left"

Tom.[11] I had pulled a muscle in a game on the previous night and I wasn't fit but I went and due to the shaky play of our backs and half-backs I got very little to do.

We were in the middle of this game when the familiar recurrent roar of Nazi planes made us look up. There were two planes, flying high, and since they swept over the harbour unmolested we concluded we must have mistaken their identity. The game went on until we heard them return. Then the Ack-Ack guns went into action. We scurried for shelter and watched. Again and again they swept across the harbour and town thru the barrage. But they were out of range and headed unscathed for home with shells cracking on their tails.

It was our first raid for weeks and I felt something of the old terror coming back. It is an intense enlivening thing the stimulus of fear. Not to have felt it in that sickening, purging gust which sweeps thru one's innards is not to have lived. The limits of Life and Death become blindingly clear and with searing clarity you see the falsity of the poet's acceptance of Death as the "Brother of Sleep".[12] It is no longer lapped in the soft, languorous shades of the imagination. It is not merely cessation of life. It is the robber of all your earthly possessions; it knows no conventions, it snatches from you the one you love; it plunders your dreams and sets them at naught; no more will you sit by your fire and read your beloved books; you wanted to be a journalist, your pen will never rouse the world, make it weep, make it laugh with you. All the deep and secret longings of your heart, dreams of love, ambitions, all are under the eraser of Death. And you can but wait for the stroke.

The danger is over before your pulse stops pounding. Then in that glorious refreshing moment of realisation you take air into your lungs and delight in the purely animal pleasure of being alive. And the vision and the glory "fade into the light of common day".[13]

I wrote a couple of poems. I managed to get something of atmosphere and flesh into them. But as usual I left them unpolished. I shall go back to them yet. If I could only sustain this creative effort I might be able to make my stuff finished enough for publication. But my notebooks are crammed with uncut, rough-hewn verses. I'm sure this indolence, this lamentable lack of concentration will prove the undoing of my literary ambitions if I don't discipline myself in time. As it is I'm finding this diary is a tremendous impetus in the right direction. For tho it does not compel the mind in any one direction, the very physical act of writing and the mental compulsion of literary expression are themselves invaluable discipline. Also the increased leisure of life in the tropics gives more encouragement for writing, tho the enervating atmosphere of this colony may offset the advantage to some considerable extent.

For four weeks there was no mail for me. Letters for others came and I had the chagrin of watching them read them over. Frankly I was worried, feeling at times in despair. But not at any time did I doubt that Betty was writing. She told me she would write twice a week and I knew there would be letters somewhere unless... It was that conditional which gave me so much pain. Was she safe? Had she perhaps been hurt and they were not informing me till she was well again. I tortured myself with all manner of ghastly possibilities. My imagination was fertile soil for such nightmares and try as I would I could not rid myself of these harpies.

Every day I would scan the face of the Post-Cpl. but it told me nothing. Nor did his habitual dry nod give me any encouragement to keep asking him.

As the summer approached the rains became more frequent, the storms more violent. When we landed here at first the margin of clouds in the night sky was lit for hours by the lightning, which flashed and darted in a magnificent extravagance of latent power and light. But there was no mutter of anger from the skies. The stars like jewels caught in a tangle of white hair were aloof and serene; the slow smooth ripple of the waters reflected them in a million exquisite coruscations. Over the bush-clad hills the purple mists hung in a wispy shawl. Then the thunder began to accompany the lightning. And last night (2nd October 1940) the mounting fury of the elements reached its crescendo in a terrific climacteric.

All the afternoon the air was sultry, not a breath stirred among the dry grasses. The vultures hung uneasily low over the roofs of our huts, and sat bunched up like brown evil fungi among the branches of the mango trees in the compound. Eyeballs flashed white in the black faces of the boys as they glanced fearfully at the sky. The sun glared down on the red ferruginous slopes, and a low line of dark cloud with frayed, surly contours appeared over the horizon's edge. The sea was a sheet of tarnished copper stretching out to where the mists brooded motionless over the swampy headland. As the afternoon progressed the masses of cloud swept up the sky like a great tidal wave; the sea deepened to an inky blue. Tamba[14] sat shivering on the end of my bed. I felt his hands and they were ice cold. Then the wind came. In little gusts, at first, which snuffled and whimpered in the caves of the hut and played fitfully with a dry leaf in the gutter. In five minutes the great broad leaves on the mop-heads of the paw-paw trees were waving wildly like banners. A window banged; then the door flew wide open with an almighty clatter, and upset a tin helmet hanging behind it. As I went out to shut the windows a great adder of lighting zipped up from the clouds' edge. Then the world seemed to crack in a terrific thunderclap, which rattled the loose planks on the veranda and set my ears ringing. A large spot of rain fell on the back of my hand; it was warm to the touch. The grey mist swept down from the mountain and the rains came in swift diagonal needles, which soon fused into a great screen of water. Frogs hopped out from beneath the hut and leapt the streaming gutters; some, falling short, were swept down in the mad spate of water, which

Jack with his Freetown chums – back row, left to right: Jack, Willie Adams, Cyril Packham, "Digger" Lees; front row: Levy

foamed and raced to the lower levels. The thunder roared and guffawed like frenetic cacodemons amongst the hills and the lightning lashed the skies with a stinging whip of fire. The wind whined and tore at the roof of our hut and bent young saplings to the ground. As we watched the heavens were split from end to end in a searing flame and even as we rubbed our blinded eyes the earth rocked in a shattering explosion, which sent us clutching one another in dismay. It was the climax. The rain sank to a sibilation and the wind to a moist whisper amongst the drenched grasses. The clouds broke apart and a star shone with a myriad scintillations in the gap. But all night long the compound was lit with recurrent flashes and the thunder continued in a subdued mutter. Dawn came with a clear sky and the sun glittered on the many-faceted raindrops clinging to the leaves. The storm was over.

When Betty's letters came, it was by spate. The 2nd, 3rd, 5th October brought mail from her. What a darling she is! Her letters and her life is so full of our home, plans for our future and all that she is doing to build our home. And I, stuck out here, seem to be so useless, so helpless to do anything to contribute to our future. Even saving money is almost impossible with the cost of living so high in the colony. But I will take home some presents or bust. I've puzzled and budgeted in an attempt to cut down extravagances. But I seem to have none! I don't drink beer (too expensive @ 1/5 per pint). My smoking is the only thing – 5/- per week and I can't seem to do with less. However, I'll figure it out somehow.

I replied to all of my letters. But oh how irksome this censorship is. To try and write a love letter for the eyes of the disinterested censor and the intensely interested beloved without seeming saccharine and fudge to the censor or aloof and cool to the loved one is more intensely difficult than I ever imagined. It's all very well to say, disregard the censor, but you are aware even subconsciously of this third party. And compromise is most unsatisfactory. The only way out I've discovered is to convey all my feelings without suppression or disguise but to attempt to frame them in as flawless a literary style as possible. It detracts from the spontaneity and it takes time but I've found no other way out.

But oh, I'm sick of the thin skilly of letters. To hell with this emasculated love! For a year we have been condemned to it, Betty and I, and now I'm longing for normal love again.

14th October 1940

> 14th Oct. 1940.
>
> Another mail came again to-day. A brief pathetic little note from Betty; rather doleful without a letter from me for 3 weeks & to make things worse a terrific cold. Poor dear! I know so well how she must be feeling. I pray she has my mail by now.

Another mail came again to-day. A brief pathetic little note from Betty; rather doleful, without a letter from me for 3 weeks & to make things worse a terrific cold. Poor dear! I know so well how she must be feeling. I pray she has my mail by now.

A letter from a friend too with all the gossip of the 157th. It was like a faint echo from the city of the living to hear from a friend who was associated with so many pleasant memories.

The 157th F.A. have a new C.O. He seems to be a man of some culture and character and a welcome change to old McGreehin.

I have never met such a "typical" bachelor as Lt. Col. J.P. McGreehin.[15] Fussy, a valetudinarian to an extreme degree, and a tee-totaller. I shall always laugh as I remember his agitated rush into the kitchen in Beaminster. "House is like a lighthouse, Chapman. Shining like a lighthouse. Come out here. See it shining on the flagstones, Chapman. Something wrong. Terrible thing this is." And when Chapman pointed out it was only the moon shining over the roof. "Yes, so it is, so it is. Most curious, Chapman. Strong moon. Isn't it a very strong moon tonight. Most extraordinary, Chapman." And he went away muttering. Then the incident of the paper, which he related so meticulously and laboriously to David. He was quite the most ineffectual man I ever met in his position.

He tells me he has some interesting incidents to relate if the letters are not censored. I expect it is more homosexuality. He was not so bad as his friend, but the streak was very marked. He was the first man of the type I ever associated with and apart from this orientation of his affections towards his own sex he was a perfectly normal and thoroughly likeable fellow.

Levy, Lees, Adams and myself had a conversation on the subject the other evening. Turning to sex as our talks invariably do, like the magnetic needle to the pole, we discussed the homosexual. Levy was prone to regard him with disgust – in his words, "To kick his arse for him". Lees opined that such men do not deserve the respect of any clean-minded person. None of them had known any actual subject as I did and as Adams professed to do. And we two described the process in some detail, showing that these were pathological and psychological cases. They are invariably more deserving of pity than of contempt. The opinions of the other two did veer a bit I think. And we were ultimately in almost complete concord. We should cast aside all the opprobrium and shame with which conventional morality has surrounded homosexuality. It is not a product of a century but common with only slight variation to all centuries. We should recognise it as one of the facts of the multiple aspects of life. It is not to be cloaked in shame because of its deviation from the norm or because of the minority of its kind.

In the course of the same conversation Lees suggested that there should be a Regimental Brothel in town, adding that in France where such places are government-controlled, the percentage of V.D. is the lowest in Europe. His statistics were wrong, diametrically so, but

74

his original suggestion had sound sense in it. There are men who need to indulge their lust and they ought to be protected for the good of their fellows. For in this colony the climate does tend to inflame the sexual desires and the boredom and lack of sublimative alternatives exaggerates it. For my own part the business of using prostitutes is utterly repugnant. Added to this is the fact that the risk of disease is not worth any dubious pleasure, which might be involved. I can't see how the sexual act can be divorced from the attendant mental associations. How can it be done in that callous, animal sort of way? In my own experience, even the desire for it I never felt till I fell in love. I couldn't do it without being in love.

Another letter from Betty even more frantic than the last. Five weeks since she had a letter!! O Christ, poor darling!! I can't imagine what can be holding my mail up. But I am glad I sent off a cable yesterday. Perhaps it will help to console her just a little. She must be wondering, perhaps not consciously, if I am writing and blaming herself for doubting. Yet she has no concrete proof of the fact. What a bloody state. Here I am writing about every second day and Betty never sees one of my letters. I give up...

There has been a great deal of talk on Russia's entry into the war on Britain's side, provoked by the German seizure of Rumania. But that act of itself constitutes no direct threat to Russia, even tho it foreshadows more drastic thrusts towards the Black Sea. Anyhow it seems highly improbable that the Nazis should so openly flout Russia's interests as to incite the vengeance of the Soviets and add this mighty neutral to the list of their enemies. Russia protested rather half-heartedly against the fact that Germany had occupied the country without notifying her first. Germany replied that Russia had been notified and the mild tiff died down. It was obvious that either Russia had been "sounded", as Britain was in her attitude to Czechoslovakia, and it had been ascertained that she would take no action, or her entire concurrence had been secretly secured and the protest was only a lame attempt to conceal her betrayal of a neighbour.

Russia's policy is certainly neutral at this stage, but that it can remain so for long is a matter for doubt. She is becoming a victim of German encirclement. But an Allied victory will save her the trouble of fighting the Nazis and in the other eventuality of the Nazis gaining the victory they will be in no position to dispute Russia's claims by force. Without some serious blunders – faults which the Nazi administration have not so far revealed – Russian neutrality is assured.

The news of America's conscription of sixteen-and-a-half million men gave us some encouragement. Tho it will take 12 months to put her in a position of providing any positive military aid to us. It is unlikely that any declaration on policy in this direction will be forthcoming until after the presidential election. Roosevelt cannot afford to commit his country to such an irrevocable step while his authority is in the electoral balance. It is nevertheless a matter for comfort that both sides in the campaign are pledged to help the British cause. Nor do I think, after the election, that this assistance will fall far short of the extreme degree in a declaration of war.

In the meantime, we are alone, trading murder for murder, destruction for destruction, terror for terror with Germany. The collapse of civilian morale in one or both sides may terminate the war before the entry of America can be fulfilled as a fact.

21ˢᵗ October 1940

Tonight we sat in a circle round the hurricane lamp singing some of the popular classics. Somehow they sloughed their hard, bandstand, gramophonic veneer. Tosti's "Farewell", Tchaikovsky's "Minuet", Schubert's "Serenade", Dvorak's "Humoresque", Gilbert and Sullivan, Mozart, Handel's "Messiah", Liszt's Rhapsodies, German, "Jerusalem". We did not sing tunefully or with exquisite attention to the score, but there was all sincerity in the volume of song and all the nostalgic throb of the stranger singing his songs in a strange land. Young men in the dim fringe of lamplight singing the old songs, dreaming the old dreams, in their hearts the old love of the homeland. Young men in the twilight throwing the old musical challenge of the centuries into the dark chasm, which is set between them and their home. Then one by one we crept away to our beds, each man to his darkness, each man to his memories.

The "Griffin" was born some days back. Some wisecracker coined the word to describe the Rumour. The Griffin is a fabulous monster. It was applied to rumour and it stuck. Now at every table in the dining hall the question is asked, "What's the Griffin today?" There is always some "pickka Griffin". "Going home by Xmas". "Home by June". "All the B-category men going home". "Fifty R.A.M.C. needed for the Hospital Ship to sail to England". There may have been a grain of truth in some, but they were all products of the universal desire to get out of this God-forsaken colony.

We were notified in Orders that the practice of paying the boys extra for boot-cleaning etc. must cease. And they are not to be used for any other purpose than that of laundry boys. The authorities are determined to keep the boys as near starvation point as possible. £1 per month to provide for a man, wife and family!! God, what beasts whites are! Is it adequate ? Is it just? Is it charitable? Is it democratic?

Consider the position of Tamba. The staple diet, rice, costs 15/- and he is unable to afford any other food to supplement this. His family totals three and the bushel only lasts one month. The rent he pays for a squalid little shack of corrugated iron sheeting is 7/6 monthly. If he fails to pay his rent the Government bailiffs take his clothes and house, sell them, and drive their owner up-country in a loincloth. His wages are according to the Government, £1 a month, his liabilities 22/6!! This is British colonisation, British enlightenment. This is the absolute value of freedom we are fighting for. This is Britain the just, Britain the righteous!!

If we obey the order we compel a man to incur debt, to starve himself and his family; we perpetuate his degradation, we drive him back into savagery. If we pay him that little extra we improve his self-respect, we encourage his ambitions, we make it possible for him to buy food and keep out of debt, but we disobey the orders and are liable to punishment. We decided unanimously on the latter course. We decided to act illegally, but to act morally.

22nd October 1940

The news reports an article in Ciano's newspaper[16] urging the cessation of hostilities and a discussion of terms. Almost simultaneously the organ of the Nazi Storm-Troopers makes tentative efforts for a compromise on peace terms. Churchill in a broadcast tells the French people, "It won't be many months now". Is it that all three powers betray a weariness of war?

Reports that the Vichy government is contemplating war against Britain. We are of the opinion that such a step might in the end be to our advantage. France will no longer be permitted to masquerade as a neutral under German tutelage. Moreover she can't have her south-west ports well enough fortified to withstand a strong attack, which was unforeseen at the inception of the war. This weak spot in the coast may be all that we need to gain foothold in France. Again, can the French Army be trusted with arms, and, if so, is its morale good enough to allow them to be effective? These points are still in abeyance.

23rd October 1940

I had a silly squabble with Levy over some bread in the dining hall!! I was using tactics to secure the best pieces of the loaf, which Levy himself was in the habit of doing. He was feeling a bit liverish, I expect, and tore the food from my fingers. I saw red for a second, and would have struck him, but I saw in time how foolish a figure I was cutting and tho the bickering and the threatening continued for some minutes I was treating the whole thing half as a joke and at last Lev. broke up and we laughed the whole thing off.

But the incident showed how degrading Army habits are & how frayed one's temper becomes in the tropics. I made a mental resolve to watch my passions more carefully. I'd hate to return to Betty bad-tempered, churlish and ill-mannered. She doesn't deserve that sort of person tied to her.

We had a discussion on birth-control in the evening. The mechanical methods we rejected as being at least emotionally unsatisfactory if not definitely harmful in that respect and in the physical also. The "safe period" we discussed in all its interpretations. Packham, giving Kent's theory, maintained substantially that no such period of non-conception exists, and if it does exist it is unpredictable. His theory was that the descent of the ovum was uncertain in occurrence and in duration, taking place often <u>during</u> menstruation. And he went on to say that its vulnerability is not greatly impaired even up to its destruction.

The theory which Adams propounded and which I am strongly inclined to adhere to, has the strongest weight of evidence behind it. The results, yielded in test cases in the U.S. as far as I remember, were 80% correct; about the remaining 10% there was some doubt owing to probable error in execution by the cases concerned. Moreover there is the legal "relevant date" during which time the law regards conception as impossible.

There is, said Adams, a space of five days between menstruation and menstruation during which conception does take place. The 10 days immediately following and immediately preceding menstruation are definitely safe. And for these reasons. The ovum is not fully descended till about 12 days after menstruation, and by allowing two days grace any sperm whose life is only 48 hours may be assumed to have died. As the days progress the ovum grows round itself a hard "shell" of albumen and becomes fairly impregnable, this process having been completed 10 days before the menstrual flow commences. This theory commends itself from every viewpoint. But why is it not more widely known? Is it being withheld for prudish or expedient reasons? That seems the only explanation.

A man I knew, I recollect, used it with effect in his affair with a girl. He was utterly immoral, unscrupulous, and his intentions towards the girl were only physical. And he told her so! But he was not the man to run his head in a noose thru ignorance or carelessness. We used to laugh him to exasperation when the woman's periods were late, but tho he worried himself stiff he came thru unscathed for 12 months. Then the appeal was wearing off. He was due to graduate and he gave her up.

25ᵗʰ October 1940

25ᵗʰ Oct. 1940. The Vichy talks with Hitler braught nothing more than vague threats. Laval seems to have been willing to go to any lengths to satisfy his German masters but there was some restraint exercised from his government. Whether they still retain some nobility of spirit or no is not clear. But they made no definite stand against Britain for the present.

The Vichy talks with Hitler brought nothing more than vague threats. Laval[17] seems to have been willing to go to any lengths to satisfy his German masters but there was some restraint exercised from his government. Whether they still retain some nobility of spirit or no is not clear. But they made no definite stand against Britain for the present.

There is news today of Hitler scampering all the way across France to meet his Spanish beneficiary, Franco, on the Pyrenees. Again nothing but "identity of views" and furious threats from Rome of, "Just wait. Spain will be on your tail very soon".

> The cicadas' chorus repeats the monotony of life in the tropics. The great fly wheel of routine turns & turns.

The cicadas' chorus repeats the monotony of life in the tropics. The great flywheel of routine turns and turns.

The mind relives only with the setting of the sun. There are two candles on my box, two golden little tears casting ripples of light in the darkness. By their light I read or write or talk with my friends as they sit within the fluid boundaries of the mellow light. Oftentimes I just dream, and my thoughts float gently on the ebb and flow of the quiet tides.

A black mamba was found by one of the men under his pillow. The creature was happily no less lethargic than the other natives of this place and without difficulty a noose was slipped over its head and made fast. It was then taken to the M.I. Room and chloroformed into harmlessness. The incident turned my mind to Lawrence's poem and Saroyan's story. I looked for the books. Both are gone! People likely to read these books are not likely to be criminal-minded. Is it only carelessness I wonder? Then, tho they may enjoy the books, they don't love them as I do. To keep another man's books is like estranging the affections of his wife. It should be equally punishable by social opprobrium.

28th October 1940

Greece is the latest victim of the murderous plague sweeping the world. One by one the smaller nations are being sucked into the vortices of war, some struggling manfully against the dreadful irrational forces which threaten to destroy them, others acquiescing in a last despairing hope that they will thus suffer less hurt.

Certain demands were made to the Greek Govt. by Italy, demands which were regarded by Metaxas[18] as a direct threat to Greek independence. These demands followed the usual Axis press campaign of vituperation, threats, allegations of un-neutral behaviour and the like, and it was plain to everyone that Greece was the next victim. But it was doubtful whether she, like Rumania and Denmark, poor Bohemia and France, would allow herself to be lured to the Procrustean bed of the Nazis' "New World Order". She resisted and everyone heaved a sigh of relief. It would have made the greatest tragedy of the war had a country with such a heritage failed to strike back for her own freedom.

But it is inconceivable still that war has come to Greece, that these emerald Archipelagos and peaceful green lands of Thrace and Attica set in the turquoise matrix of the Mediterranean should hear the shout of guns and all the evil clangour of modern mass murder. Over Athens now the bombers roar, echoing in the market place, which once rang with the oratory of Pericles and Demosthenes. Perhaps there are bombs crashing on the time-limned Doric columns of Pheidias' immortal temple of Olympus. But no clamour of war will drown the whisper of reason and sanity and freedom, which still lingers in the quiet gardens of the Academy where Socrates talked and Plato, and the Peripatetics argued and wrote. The voices of Greece's past, the song of Homer and Sappho, the grim jest of Euripides and Aristophanes, the tragic masques of Aeschylus, the histories of Thucydides, the voices of Demosthenes and Pericles, of Socrates and Plato and Solon and Archimedes. These will never be stilled as long as men thrill to poetry and to oratory, as long as wonder stirs in their hearts and their governments are subject to change.

The question now at issue is, "Will Britain send effective and <u>timely</u> help?" Surely there will be no repetition of the Norwegian and Dakar debacles.

So the shuttle of the days moves over the great loom of history. In boredom and excitement, laughter and tears we strike day after day from our calendar. The insidious buzz of rumour is ever in our ears.

Man of Shadows

You man of shadows, you skulker
In rank passageways, man of grey visage,
Man with the fugitive eyes, and
Shoulders folded like black wings,
Fumbling with white fingers
Over the braille of empty sockets.
Of doors and damp-ridged lamp-posts –
What you seek dwells not within walls
Nor in this stained boulevard of gas-lamps.
Here at the end of this street only hell-blooms
Roseately flourish in their iron matrices
And the lavish palaver of production
Fills night with enormous derision;
Pasty women heckle at the iron gates
And a spasm of light crosses their faces
Like a wan rat, phthisic-pale, and fleers off
Back into the gloom. This is not the path,
This iron cul-de-sac, O grey one
With the searching eyes. The fact is
You are no adventurer. Seeking you came
From a darkness to a darkness with bewildered eyes
And no dialectic compass to scrutinise
And blunder to a makeshift habitat. No familiar voice
Makes a trusty handhold in this ravine of dying echoes.
And you are lost. Alone. Starless.

Reflect your temerity, vagabond spirit.
Repent not. Salvation lies not in negative
Back-tracking to the Fork. Search always
And not regret. Press always forward
Breasting the flotsam of the dark unflinching.
Stretch the ligaments. Tear. Advance. Fail.
Take counsel of – the puddle-mirror
Corrugates. The grey man, man of shadows
Fades off the screen: my mind is a derelict projector
With no light. And No star makes
Golden hints in the rain-wet street.

III

Moving
November 1940 to May 1941

By the end of October, the Battle of Britain had been won by RAF Fighter Command and Germany's plans for an all-out invasion of Great Britain had been crushed. The so-called "Battle of Britain Day", on September 15, which had seen the RAF tear into the enormous incoming Luftwaffe formations in the skies above London and the south coast, proved a decisive blow for Hitler, who, despite wreaking great havoc from the air for almost four months with what on paper appeared to be a superior air force in numbers of planes, pilots and experience, was forced to accept that his grand designs of bringing Britain to heel had taken a disastrous turn. By the battle's end, the RAF had lost some 1,000 aircraft, the Luftwaffe around 1,700. Churchill's victorious refrain – "Never... was so much owed by so many to so few" – remains one of the defining moments of this long 114-day aerial encounter, which brought Britain back from the brink.

Moving into early 1941, and "Glasgow has been effectively blitzed" was Jack's sober pronouncement on a German attack by air that centred on Clydebank. On the nights of March 13 and March 14, the Luftwaffe bombed this sturdy little industrial town, just seven miles from the centre of Glasgow, to within an inch of its existence. Key to the Allied war-effort for its production of ships and munitions, Clydebank was a natural target for the German Luftwaffe and this hardworking burgh was forced to withstand two full nights of German aerial bombardments. On the first night, 236 German bombers attacked targets in the Clydebank area, such as Singer's Sewing Machine factory, which was charged with making munitions. Over 200 Luftwaffe bombers returned the following night, also attacking targets in the Glasgow vicinity, which housed the likes of the Rolls Royce Aero Engine factory in Hillington Industrial Estate. Kilmun Street, in Glasgow's Maryhill, felt the full might of the Luftwaffe's rage when it was set ablaze. By the end of the raid, more than 1,200 people had been killed in the Clydeside area, and the destruction in Clydebank proper was so devastating that over 35,000 of its some 50,000 residents were left homeless. Other Scottish cities and towns to suffer at the hands of the Luftwaffe during the Second World War, included Peterhead, Aberdeen and Fraserburgh. But none were bloodier than the Clydebank Blitz, which claimed the lives of more than 500 men, women and children in the town itself.

"I was morose and irritable and enthusiastically defeatist," writes Jack in the grim aftermath of the bombing in which it was reported that only seven of Clydebank's 12,000 houses escaped harm.

By the end of 1940, Jack's attention to dating his diary entries was on the slide, and, in general, for the rest of his time in Freetown, he settled for making little more than off-hand references to the passing months in his written accounts of life in the tropics. This shift, which he put down in a later diary entry to his effectively living in a perpetual state of oblivion – as if the days and weeks merged into one long infinite passage of time – was understandable such was the nature of his work and the nature of his posting in a city, which Greene had described – somewhat tellingly – as possessing "a Bret Harte[19] air without the excitement, the saloons, the revolver shots or the horses".[20]

It was, perhaps, fortunate then that in early 1941, he was asked to present himself at the city's local university for a few short stints as an English Literature lecturer. Described by Jack in his introduction as the "best experience" of his one-year and four months in the colony, his brief spell in Fourah Bay College forever associated him with a celebrated part of West African history, which began in 1827 when the college was founded by the Church Missionary Society (CMS) – a British Anglican organisation with strong links to the Society for the Abolition of the Slave Trade – in the Sierra Leone capital. Established to turn out African missionaries and teachers for the CMS's evangelical work in West Africa, Fourah Bay acquired degree-granting powers in 1876 when it succeeded in becoming a constituent college of England's Durham University, and it delivered its first female graduate in 1938. Fourah Bay College, the oldest university college in West Africa, is today under the auspices of the University of Sierra Leone, and is currently a member of the Tony Blair Faith Foundation's Faith and Globalisation Initiative, the former British prime minister's link to the college dating back to his own father who taught law in the halls of Fourah Bay during the 1960s.

Jack's brief reference to "Syrians" in an earlier entry is also touched upon as he describes his encounter with one jungle-weary soldier – not *unlike those so referenced by author John Harris as prone to losing the plot due to inactivity in his partially autobiographical novel of Second World War Sierra Leone,* A Funny Place to Hold a War *– who floats a plan to flee the army by masquerading as a Syrian immigrant. Such a plan almost certainly had its roots in the number of "Syrians" – or, to be more accurate, Lebanese – who made their home in Sierra Leone and all across West Africa after a silkworm crisis struck Ottoman Lebanon in the mid-19th century. Historical records put the 1890s as the point at which the first Lebanese settlers began arriving on the shores of Sierra Leone. Today, 6,000 to 7,000 Lebanese reside in the West African state – though far less than in the 1960s – with Freetown itself having long since established a reputation as a city brimming with businesses owned and run by Lebanese entrepreneurs.*

For Jack at least, and as far as this wartime predicament was concerned, his colleague's plot was nothing short of fantasy.

"I almost laughed aloud at the absurdity of the scheme," he notes with undisguised bemusement.

Enemy Bombers Raided a Town

Bury thy dead, O cities
And let thy tears fall
Into the common grave. Earth pities
And will accept for them
This last gift of all.

Do thou pity those
Who dwell in new silences
And listen at the day's close
For known footfalls on empty stairs
In empty rooms for dead voices.

Spare thou them the praise
And eulogy which smears remembrance
Of the private dead. Raise
No pallid plinth to glamorise
Their evil chance.

They died by door and hearth
Busied with domestic decencies, not
In disciplined ranks where was no dearth
Of candidates for death. Yet they bore
Like veterans their stranger-lot.

Those who love them live
Without thanksgiving.
No stars burn in the gulf
And a grey patina settles
Over all their living.

Diary

4th November 1940

> 4th Nov. 1940. There was a concert to-night given by some of our men. There was tremendous excitement in the air previous to it, a general sort of gala spirit.

There was a concert to-night given by some of our men. There was tremendous excitement in the air previous to it, a general sort of gala spirit.

The stage was an improvised affair of tabletops and trestles, the wings and curtains comprised of old blankets sewn together. A lame attempt was made to introduce "song sheet" community singing but the men would have none of it. Someone started "Our Sergeant-Major" and the whole gamut of ribaldry was sung thru with the band feeling its way along behind. The officers entered with the sisters and there were cries of, "A-she-moo", followed by a loud guffaw. The sisters were preserved specimens of that Empire-building race of maiden ladies led by Florence Nightingale. All were over 40 and none looked as if she had been "neglected".

The compere, Lane, a long horse-faced fellow with a lugubrious humour had a Sunday-school-soiree manner and was greeted on every entry with mock laughter, which he apparently accepted as genuine appreciation. The turns were nondescript, limping sketches and monologues which thru not being pushed thru with sufficient slickness and gusto simply left the audience cold. Paddy O'Connor squeezed the "Rose of Tralee" thru his teeth, and gave such a lamentable performance that some malicious spirits encored him. He only got halfway thru the encore when the wave of cheering brought him a merciful exit. The band was adequate and played bravely and the whole thing ended in a riot of cheering. Nobody enjoyed the performance, but everyone had a good time. It is always so with Army concerts. The majority go not to listen, but to let off a lot of concerted steam and having done so, they leave quite satisfied.

The Greeks have pushed the enemy back about eight miles into Albania, capturing a large amount of equipment and a few tanks. British troops have landed and the R.A.F. are co-operating with the Greek Air Force. On the whole the position looks brighter for Greece than for any of the other nations we have guaranteed. But we must beware of optimism and accept everything only as a "temporary statement". When we begin to hear of "strategic withdrawals" we shall know that all is up. Meanwhile we are holding our breath and hoping...

We have been told to pack and be ready to move over to Wilberforce, on the other side of the town, by 8 a.m. tomorrow. We all have a foretaste of what it will be like to pack for home and it sends a thrill thru us. Then about 12 midnight comes the news, "Move cancelled meanwhile". Levy says, "Why don't the bleeders make up their bloody minds?" That was the question we were all asking. Why make all these elaborate arrangements and then discover that they didn't work? This, I suspect, is the way the war is being run also.

5th November 1940

Again the order to move. This time there was no cancellation. We loaded the truck with our belongings and hanging our pots on the tailboard we set off like a mechanised gipsy caravan.

The approach to Wilberforce is undeniably arresting. When the road emerges from the tangle of the native dwellings it crosses the broad gully of a stream diminished now to a few little runlets and rock-hemmed gushes; here, the native women, bare-breasted, shrill-voiced, wash their clothes, beating them between two flat stones. Thru a green cool arch of trees and once again you traverse a narrow road skirting the little inland lake. It is oyster-shaped, palm-fringed, a mirror of turquoise whose surface is not disturbed by the fishing boats, which, like little brown moths, drift towards the shores. Turning from the sea the road bends and twists thru burnt scabrous wastes of scrub and grassland, thru cool mango-groves where the spiders are busy in the sunlight, and gossamer hangs like silver on the leafy cornices. Rising and turning the whole tropical diorama lies bathed in the golden tranquillity of the mid-day sun. The palms, tall, haughty sentinels rising from the green welter of vegetation on the slopes; the little lake we passed glows in the exquisite emerald bowl of the eminencies, which surround it. Thickly wooded isthmuses stretch out to the sea their green arms lined with the tawny sand, which the tongue of white surf licks greedily. The thunder of the waves reaches us in an intermittent murmur. Beyond it all the moveless blue sea and the silver-blue haze of the sky. It is a picture executed by an impulsive child with a new paint-box – rich splashes of ultramarines and yellows and vermilions and Prussian blues.

The Camp lies in a little depression on the plateau. It is surrounded by a thick bank of trees, which obscures the sea. It is an unhealthy, uninteresting, soul-less military barracks.

We moved in, hung our pictures, arranged our furniture – and shifted to another barrack-room the following day!

On our arrival we went slap on the wards. I landed in the Surgical Section and retired at 8 p.m. weary and disgusted. I little thought I should ever have to submit to such menial, nauseating work – sweeping wards, dishwashing, purveying bedpans and urinals. Foh!

> I went to the R.S.M. about some more congenial job but was put off in the usual vague Army way. Later in the week I made another attempt which met with a similar rebuttal. I gave up.

I went to the R.S.M. about some more congenial job but was put off in the usual vague Army way. Later in the week I made another attempt which met with a similar rebuttal. I gave up.

The future lay before me, a dismal projection of the present. I went to bed tired and dejected, in no mood for intellectual exercise of any sort. At 5:30 a.m. we rose in a melancholy grey dawn touched with crimson. The physical training at 5:45 a.m. was gone thru grudgingly and spiritlessly. It seemed such a needless hardship to add to our already hard lot. By 6:25 a.m. we were ready for inspection and at 6:30 a.m. back to work. Women are relentless drivers and we got no rest. Errand-boys, ward-maids, of less account than servants, we were treated as useless interlopers. It was a humiliating position to be placed in and if it were not sheer thoughtlessness it was a gross psychological error. However women have deserved sex-equality, there is another factor to be considered in their place in any institution where men are working. That factor is psychological – perhaps lies in the world-old attitude of men towards women, the attitude that women are now fighting to destroy. I grant them their equality of opportunity, and even with some reserve their equality of intellectual ability, but try as I may I refuse to admit their right to direct tyranny over grown men. There is something in it, which makes conflict inevitable. And the friction is not lessened by the youthfulness of the sisters in question and their reputed moral lapses.

But the days are swift in their passage and we take comfort from the hours, which lie behind us never to be relived.

About the beginning of December I became acquainted with Smith. A L/Cpl in the Essex Regiment he came into hospital complaining of headaches. He'd had a slight attack of malaria, but there was no trace of it in his blood stream when he came under my care. However, he never appeared to me to be anything near so bad as he professed to be. His head was x-rayed and showed slight opacity in the antrum and ethmoid regions, nothing but what might have been ascribed to a catarrhal cold. I guessed he was swinging the lead and he later confessed to it. But considering the arduous routine of the Essex training I was not surprised at such a thing. The M.O. most certainly knew of many such cases and obligingly connived at them.

Why of all the patients I tended I have taken to Smith more than any other is as inexplicable as all the other casual acquaintances which one makes and then finds mysteriously ripen into friendship.

He had a frank round face with ruddy cheeks and a firm chin. The small deep-set eyes rather seemed to contradict the impression of cherubic candour, but nothing in his conduct or conversation ever confirmed the sinister hint in the eyes. He was tall and his limbs like his face were smooth and rounded rather than rugged with muscles. His whole aspect suggested the large over-grown boy, and the tiny crinkling of the eyes and nose when he smiled were pleasantly child-like. He had a defect of speech, which was a halt rather than a stutter, but he was in no way self-conscious of it for he would take part in the most involved discussion without a qualm. He had a certain charming naiveté in his manner, a directness and lack of subtlety, which attracted me. He would ask all kinds of questions about his ailments, actual and possible, and I suppose I was flattered in finding someone who expected me to know something. Out of my threadbare knowledge of medicine I told him as best I could. Then one day in a gust of self-confidence he told me, "Look here I've got to get home, somehow, anyhow. If you knew my position you'd understand. Can you help me?" I replied that if I knew a way of getting out of here I should try it myself. "Don't try 'working your ticket' here," I said. "The M.O. is no fool and he'll twig you right away."

"I must do it somehow," said Smith. "I can't stand this any longer." And he plunged into a whispered history of his life and origins. He was an orphan pushed around from relative to relative, left avuncular care at 16 and joined the Army from which he was discharged (he says), "for being indifferent". He married at 18, has a child and seems fairly happy with his family. As he explained his life, emphasising his homelessness, and his lack of proper affection in the past, it was easy to see how much his own home, wife and child must mean to him. Always in his childhood and in his adolescence he was an intruder, now there was a woman who loved <u>him</u>, a child of his, and a home, which <u>he</u> had made. They were like the symbols of his hard-won independence and his first personal possessions. They meant more to him than the ill reports of the world; he was prepared to dodge, lie and cheat for their sake.

He had a plan. He proposed to disguise himself as a Syrian, get into Dakar and act the saboteur. It was mad and I told him so. He agreed and said, "I shall put it before the O.C., even take it to the Brigadier, and one of three things will happen. (1) They will send me, (2) Consider me a nuisance and send me on escort duty back to England or (3) Label me wrong in the mind and send me home. In the first case I shall be doing something active, and if I bring it off they may give me some leave. Secondly, when I get home I won't come back. Thirdly, I shall probably get out of the Army."

I almost laughed aloud at the absurdity of the scheme and its childish conclusions, but he was so manifestly earnest, and so pathetically depending on my serious consideration that I stifled my amusement and tried as gently as possible to dissuade him. But I had hardly begun when he interrupted me with a question so irrelevant it surprised me. "You may be a writer some day," he broke in. "Will you include me in one of your books?" And all thru that conversation he changed course as surprisingly and decisively every few minutes. It was impossible to give continuity to anything you might discuss. Nor did he ever resume any talk of his project. Somehow he seemed like a man in great haste to be off, yet driven to secure information on a number of subjects before he went. He was not mad, but there was something of that swift flash of irrelevance in his conversation, which we find in "Hamlet". Probably his condition had something akin to that of the mournful Dane.

Later, mysteriously, his temperature shot up to about 104. His body came out in great spots, which spread their diameter till they covered him in a uniform hectic flush. I remembered in a flash he'd talked to me of trichloroethylene poisoning, telling me it had been diagnosed as scarlet fever, asking if he could get home with <u>that</u>. It was a coincidence too striking to be overlooked that the M.O. diagnosed him first as S.F. then changed his mind and wrote him off as N.Y.D. later confirmed to streptococcal infection. I asked Smith how he'd given himself this. He replied that it had just come on. For seven days I "specialled" him in Isolation and I got no explanation. His conversation was as erratic as ever, his mind as like a flea.

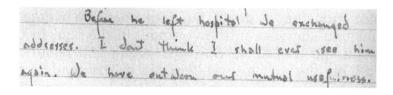

Before he left hospital we exchanged addresses. I don't think I shall ever see him again. We have outworn our mutual usefulness.

*   *   *

Work on the wards from grey dawn to starlit evening. The perpetual jog trot and the nausea of menial tasks. The insistent soprano treble and the stigma of female jurisdiction. Outside, the blue sky and the blue sea and the far-off hush-HUSH of the waves. The azaleas dropping petals, and the acacias flaming on the hillside. Inside, the faint ammoniac smell of fevers and the pungencies of the medicine cupboard. The greyish crackle of coughs in the long white wards, coughing and the weary bulge of sick bodies. Sickness in rows, tabulated, specimens. The humiliating whine of sick voices and the helplessness. Chained to autumnal humanity, ministering to pallid impotence. And the marrow-weariness, the ache along the bone. Spirit-numbness, expense of spirit in a waste of shame. The hoar brain-frost and the grey resignation and the spreading splaying lassitude. The walk to barracks under the stars and the known firmness of bed. Dropping, drugging sleep and oblivion, the anaesthesia against the grey routine of tomorrow…

*　　　　　*　　　　　*

It was death during these days, but we had not the courage to complete it, nor the power to bring life to destroy it.

*　　　　　*　　　　　*

Sister Houston is dead. Suddenly her life went. In the morning she was on the veranda, in the sun. In the afternoon she was dead. She was young and beautiful. They tell me she was not lovely in death. The dead do not bear any relation to the living. Miss Houston is gone and the thing in the morgue is only a female corpse.[21]

*　　　　　*　　　　　*

Christmas. We breakfasted well and had a faultless Xmas dinner. I had a lovely telegram from Betty. Everyone

The war graves at Freetown's King Tom Cemetery

SISTER
JANE MARGARET HOUSTON
Q.A.I.M.N.S.
12TH DECEMBER 1940

Sister Houston is buried in Freetown's King Tom Cemetery

went to bed in various stages of intoxication. Thus we celebrated Xmas. The outer forms and semblances were present, the ritual of a well-filled belly and a light head. But our hearts were cold, for home was far away. For me, Betty was not there and festivity was a hollow farce, laughter a grimace.

The initiation of our return to Mt Aureol had been made before Xmas. But we were still all together on Xmas day, and moving seemed as far off as before. Then in the week intervening between Xmas and New Year most of the Scots tipplers were quietly moved to Mt Aureol in the pretext of being an advance party. Meanwhile, we hung on and New Year's Eve arrived. We had some beer. Digger and I quietly went off to bed. There was a great deal of noise in the barrack-rooms, however, and sleep was impossible. I slung my feet over the edge of the bed and lit a cigarette. Digger, apparently sleepless also, came along and we talked quietly in the shadowy room. Talking of past New Years, of days long gone, but not easily forgotten, wondering, rather sadly, about the future, wondering what discomforts and dangers and separations were still buried in the womb of time. Somewhere the grotesque echo of maudlin laughter, then silence and a voice, very thick, insisting, "it's twelve o'clock". Then untunefully, "Auld Lang Syne". Digger and I stood up.

"Well Mac Rillie... if we can have as Happy a New Year as we've had before this do..."

"I hope to God we can, Dig," I said. We shook hands and grinned rather sheepishly and Digger went back to his bed.

I was settling down again when Jock Traill stomped into the barrack-room leading a group of Scots as drunk as he was. He brandished a corkless bottle of White Horse. "A bluidy guid New Year tae ye a'," he called. No one answered. He took a pull on the bottle and handed it round. "Ye shower o' English b------ds," he stormed and overturned a bed, sending the disgruntled occupant sprawling on the floor. Half a dozen more beds met the same fate, and then he came to mine.

Betty, February 6, 1941

I lifted my mosquito net, grabbed his hand, pumping it vigorously and insisting, "Happy New Year, Jock, Happy New Year".

"Same to you, Rillie. You're a Scotsman. Muck a' they muckin English b-----ds".

"Sure, muck them all," says I, and the stocky fair-haired, blue-eyed, Gaelic angel of destruction passed on.

In the noisy, cursing aftermath accompanying the restoration of beds to their proper positions I lay awake. I thought of the cold agonising journey thru the fog from Innerleithen last New Year's Day, Gibson's the previous year and 48 and 321. Of Mrs Macs on our first New Year together. On that note I fell asleep and dreamed blissfully of carpets and leaping fires and sherry and Betty on the arm of my chair...

Gradually, during the fortnight following, the unit transferred patients and personnel to Aureol. I was left as a member of the rear-party and when at last my own ward had gone I went on N.D. in the "Joint". I was a bit prudish about it and not a little disgusted. Further, I had on me what I took to be a heavy cold. But the pain in my head got worse in spite of 30 gm aspirin per day. My temperature would not go up during the day and they refused to admit me to hospital. Finally, it got so bad that I couldn't stand up. I sent word to the M.I. Room. No doctor available. I told S/Sgt. Smith I couldn't go on duty that night. My muscles were beyond my control, I shook from head to foot with spasms of rigor. I was shivering and burning and my head felt as tho there were burning flatirons inside turning and turning. I slept fitfully, but in the morning I felt better tho weak and still light in the head. That day we moved to Aureol. The next day I was back on the wards. And gradually the malaise was wearing off. If it wasn't malaria I had then my great-aunt is a chimpanzee! Maybe I'm tough!

The wards were more restful to the eye, but the disposition of dispensaries, labs, stores etc, made the feet ache like blazes in the consequent running about.

I heard of a vacancy in the dispensary, and asked for an interview. Refused by the R.S.M. Then suddenly, without

"War is Hell"

any warning, the clouds broke. The C.O. sent for me.

"You're a bookish sort of fellow, Rillie. We're needing a man to run the library and take charge of the patient records room, d'you think you'd like the job?"

I'm sure I <u>shouted,</u> "Yes" to him. And there I was. I worked the week out, then started on the books. At that time we had only about 500, now there are something like 2,000. I could see the Padre had no ideas on how to counteract losses or frame rules or indeed do anything but sit on a box and make rapid comments on books he had enjoyed, revealing, incidentally, an appalling lack of taste in literature. I drew up and wrote out a set of rules and presented them to the C.O. who approved them and had them typed. My next job was on the books themselves. The existing catalogue was a scrappy, haphazard affair, but I contrived, after a few days work, to discover that a quarter of the library had been lost. These losses I cut and started a new cataloguing system. The library opened and ran smoothly. No flaws have been apparent in the system and out of the 1,500 books issued to date only two have been lost, and these have been paid for by the culprits.

The important thing about the job was that it meant a measure of soul-emancipation and opportunities of self-expression. I foresaw the production of short stories, poems, possibly even the beginnings of a novel. For the first few weeks I worked undisturbed except for the daily visit of the Padre. He chattered unendingly and had the most respectable cliché ideas on everything. His mind was scrubbed white like a wooden platter, and as deep. Gradually I found him insufferable, and when he came in I retreated spiritually, turning on and off my knowing smile, answering negatively or affirmatively, queried Oh? with lifted eyebrows and thought of smacking his skinny little bottom. I grew to dread these visits, intruding with so little return on one's loneliness of thought.

But the days went by pleasantly enough. I read voraciously. I enjoyed the different feel of bindings. There was no domineering supervision, no cramping sense of de-personification. I felt free again, an individual, a creator almost. The rains were gone. The daily sky was blue, powder blue on the horizon. The night sky curded

Copy of letter to Secy. of Debating Union.

7.

Dear Sir,

Your communication of 25th March has just been discovered for me from a pile of clerical debris. I must thank you warmly for your invitation to speak to the Debating Club. Unfortunately however, duty claims me until 7.15 every day of the week except Wednesdays & Sundays. I would urge you therefore to secure another speaker to fill the date. I regretted deeply being balked of my opportunity of speaking on the last occasion as, being a Scotsman, I have many old scores against "the Englishman" which could have been wiped off gleefully on a public platform. Now again the cup of revenge is snatched from my lips! "How all occasions do inform against me"

Regretfully,

yours,

John A McKillin

7.

A typically witty note from Jack to the secretary of the debating club

104

with stars; the moon shed an unreal kind of daylight, petrified everything, mummified the ghostly flowers, lay on rooftops and on the ground like a frost. It was the light of a dying world, of mid-star spaces, of the first dawn. The air was soft and fragrant with musk and piled grass. There was rest, it was another life there under those moons, and you could look back on the other life and things which had been obscure were made clear and the insoluble resolved itself. These were the nights. The days were arid and airless, shining and sterile, devitalising yet quickening to the imagination. Life is abundant so that death is swallowed up in it. The cotton tree drops its leaves, today it is bare, tomorrow or the next day it will be clotted with green again.

We play tennis, bathe, all in a kind of physical fury – a kind of flagellation. We must crush, stifle, drown the promptings of our blood. When I am alone, longing surges within me, sings in my ears, mists my vision. Betty is far, unbearably far from me. What must I do to be saved? Again, the pat answer, for there is no alternative for me, and the answer to my needs is with her, and she is not here. It all burdens the nerves and makes one irritable. Probably Betty is feeling the strain too, maybe it is worse for her in the constant association with familiar objects.

This is Symons's book, "The Quest for Corvo": "that cold white candent voice which was more caustic than silver nitrate, and more thrilling than a scream"; "miscellaneous multitudes paved the spaces with tumultuous eyes". This book is what might be called "inside dope" on the apparatus of literary research. It is as thrilling as any adventure story with exceedingly well-spaced climaxes and their ingeniously worked ascents. Rolfe, Rose, Austin, Baron Corvo were aliases concealing four personalities contained in the brilliant, mean, unsophisticated, bitter person of Frederick William Rolfe. Rejected as a priest, despised for his financial depravity, feared for his caustic wit; unsuccessful as an artist, dismissed as a competent amateur with arresting nuance of vision, but not more than an amateur; frustrated as an inventor, dogged by lack of patronage and sheer bad fortune; as a writer, Lylyesque, Pateresque, lacking in breadth of outlook, ivory carving with his material sharpened to a knife edge; the scalpel of the surgeon rather than of the painter is apparent in his incisive sentences. He is a master of the paragraphic tour-de-force. The sordid meanness, the sudden brilliance like the flash of light on a sword blade, the dogged persistence, the remarkable fecundity of his imagination, the folly of his self-delusion and the impotence of his snarling rages when he emerged from the world of his wish into the chill atmosphere of reality, his poverty, the chances that were proffered and lost, the chances that never came his way, the beautiful refinement and "frost-bite" of his writing – all these things combine to make the gradual unfolding of the Odyssey of this strange, rare spirit an adventure in reading and an experience of the highest worth. He always failed to grasp even a portion of "this sorry scheme of things entire",[22] and constantly regarded what could only have been a desire on his part as the accomplished factual action of someone else. On more than one occasion this unfortunate penchant was his downfall. He was misunderstood, but never did anything to dispel the reputation, even went to the length of fostering it, then spat his venom on his friends when they shunned him. Yet he was a genius, a genius without the ability to be human – he was not great in his faults. He had not Marlowe's zest for Bacchus, nor Byron's joie d'amour, nor Moore's salacity, nor Wilde's perversion. His faults were vulgar, civilized meannesses – he did not pay his landlords, he "welched", he betrayed the secrets of his friends in print. His lusts were timid tentative excursions to the apartments of harlots. Yet life has a full proportion of oxymoron and thru all the mud there gleamed unmistakably the gold.

*　　　　*　　　　*

Glasgow has been effectively blitzed. I waited in great trepidation for the cable from Betty. Days passed and it did not arrive. I was nearly beside myself. Then at last it came announcing a change of address, but "all

Copy of letter to Principal, Fourah Bay Coll.

~.

Dear Sir,

Maj. MacGraith has approached me with tentative proposals to furnish some further lectures this coming term. ¶ I intimated to him that I should be glad to renew acquaintance with your students. Shakespeare, that being more of a penchant than a forte (perhaps) with me, I am willing to interpret again. If however there are any other topics within the syllabus of English literature which you would prefer me to discuss I shall do my best to concur in so far as sufficiently material is available.

Perhaps you could let me know your requirements put port or better still, name a day & hour for me to call on you (whether be either a Wednesday or Sunday)? Meantime I await your convenience.

faithfully yours,
John Smith.

~.

A letter from Jack to the principal of Fourah Bay College

safe". It did something, but not everything to lessen the anxiety, which has become a mental habit. O God, I was driven nearly to prayer in the weeks that followed! How absurdly unjust it is, how pathetically, tragically ludicrous to be evacuated from the neighbourhood we had enlisted to defend! That worry was carried with me as a vague uneasiness whose origin, on occasions, I was unable to determine. Then seeking further, I knew and recognised it, and settled down to a steady session of the blues. My work went to pieces, and has not completely recovered yet. I was morose and irritable and enthusiastically defeatist.

The letter came. Four letters came. I opened them in the library, and read, and all the pent-up distress and anxiety of these long weeks released itself in a flood of uncontrollable weeping. I was reading the first letter, and suddenly I knew I was crying. I locked the door. With every letter I opened, the tears renewed themselves. I could not stop reading, it helped me to share, in a shadowy sort of way, the sufferings of the people at home. How brave these letters were, not consciously either. God, I was proud PROUD (in capitals) of my wife! I wept, thrilled in my very soul, gladdened, sorrowful, afraid, triumphant, I wept. It was truth and beauty as I never faced it in art, as I now know because it is found only in life, so I wept and the room was filled suddenly with the last gold of the sundowning. I was distraught, bewildered and then there was release and an infusion of life and an acquisition of pride. I squared my shoulders, and faced the world in this primrose room splashed with books.

That anxiety recurred but never with such disintegrating force. I came out on the other side with shuddering memories, but I was not overcome. Perhaps reading this in later years, or even in later months, I shall seem to have made Ossa out of a wart. But the appalling proportions of the tragedy that overhung me dwarfed me into impotent insignificance. Granted, the distorting glass of distance and a sick imagination, the immensity of the thing could not have been reduced for me.

*   *   *

They've appointed me L/Cpl, probably for the quite irrelevant reason that I lectured Shakespeare at the local university – which perpends a tale. Candidly, I reckon it's about time I was recognised. Not that I crave power in the Army. I don't. It involves a great deal, a nauseatingly great deal, of what is locally known as "arse-licking". And I become quite violent whenever I am confronted with the Army penal code – the histrionic gravity of the prosecuting officer, the formal statements of the charging N.C.O. and his two unwilling witnesses, the farce of deliberation, the question to the prisoner, "Have you anything to say", and during the defence the sense that the prosecutor is flipping a coin as to whether it should be seven days or a pay stoppage. Bah! Anyhow, I am not a bricklayer, nor a miner, nor a scavenger, and they have presented me – after a grave and dignified preamble, which was an incoherent farrago of Kings Regs. and Rudyard – with one stripe, hoping I would carry the responsibility honourably!!! "Muckin' 'ell, Bill," as Levy would comment.

My chronology is beginning to bucket and skid. I'm afraid I omitted to mention a few score pages on the lectures I gave at Fourah Bay College.

Major Maegraith sent for me, told me the Padre had given him to understand I had an honours degree in English Literature. Did I think I was capable of taking a class of B.A. students on Shakespeare? Having had the insufferable technique of lecturers thrust upon me for so long I knew I could do better with little effort. I said I should be charmed to take the class. I read the texts of "Hamlet" and "Twelfth Night" for a fortnight beforehand, and went prepared to talk the heads off any congregation of undergrads. I had what was to be my first lecture on "Hamlet" carefully prepared. A nourishing paper with a level of wit. To my horror and disappointment the class consisted of one member taking "Hamlet" for one hour, the remainder "Twelfth Night" for the following period. I talked amiably to Mr Aderinola for his session, found him studious and earnest. But the class to follow cast a shadow over my mind.

Well, I bluffed thru it. Asked the class questions and criticised them, turning the lecture into a debate, in which I was chairman. I said, "Malvolio is the most truly tragic figure Shakespeare ever drew". There was an awful silence, that stupefied incredulous silence which must confront a man who might make the statement, "God is a fake", in St Paul's Cathedral. It was a nation-wide intake of breath. Then orthodoxy uprose in its fury. My voice cut thru their protests, "Good afternoon gentlemen", and I walked out.

I had tea with the principal and Thomas, one of the tutors – a frugal meal of bread, butter and jam, and that kind of apology for a bare larder which subtly suggests that the scarcity is its normal condition. Principal Roberts is of medium height, with an emaciated frame and a slight stoop. His face is long and sallow and has great shadowed hollows. A pair of immensely bright grey eyes twinkle from either side of an immense bird-like nose. A swathe of lank brown hair lies over the long rectangular skull, which, in conversation, is smoothed, from left to right, with a long fingered delicate hand. His manner does not belie the hint of his prominent nose. Hesitant, bird-like in its approaches and gestures. When he speaks a little curve of foam creams the corner of his mouth, the testament of his excitability. Of Welsh extraction, he graduated at Kings where he secured Greats in Classics. The colony has taken its toll on his nerves, exaggerating all his gestures and making conversation a mere nervous trick.

The tutor is a mouse. A colourless, bespectacled, slight individual who giggles excessively.

A pleasant reminder – I was addressed as "Mr" Rillie. Shades of normality!!

A pleasant reminder – I was addressed as "Mr" Rillie. Shades of normality!!

                    *   *   *

Reading Claude Houghton's "Chaos is Come Again".

"In some ages men believe in their destiny; in others they don't... Today, people don't believe in their destiny – or in anything else".

"Hatred is only a passionate denial of something in ourselves".

"... there's a general idea prevalent that people are more comfortable then they used to be – and happier. It's odd that their faces don't show it yet. Still, it's put forward as a justification of the machine-age. I should have thought that a man's feelings were the test – not what he has. If he feels that his life, his dreams, his struggles, his sorrows have meaning, then he's happy in the sense that things are real to him. But if he feels that his life is meaningless, it doesn't matter if he's well-housed, well clothed, has a car and all the other things in the long list of modern essentials".

"It, (a book) defines civilisation as merely an increased capacity for receiving impressions..."

"... half our vitality is expended in rendering ourselves immune to the clang and clamour of a world which is rapidly becoming one gigantic factory. Those who crack under the strain are labelled neurotic or eccentric..."

"... as it's only delicate instruments which react to the vibrations of the ether surrounding them, it is possible that eccentric people are more truly representative of this age – being more aware of it – than those who go to their graves unperturbed by any disturbance which does not adversely affect their own interests".

"That is glamour. It is independent of sex and more fundamental than magnetism".

A variation on "Jonathan Scrivener" and almost as good. Sensitive handling and acute insight into his characters. An informed, sympathetic delineator of human motives and human difficulties. I hesitate to place his literary antecedents, but I should say he lives just downstairs from Charles Morgan. His people are empirical in their approach to life; he chooses intellectuals for their higher sensitivity to the elements of life.

The quotations are chosen for personal applications and implications rather than to illustrate Mr Houghton's literary style, which is orthodox and unobtrusive. An unfortunate and rather irritating tendency he evinces is to repeat in almost identical language psychological explanations whenever the contact between two characters recurs.

I could read many more of his works even tho the "magnetic-field" arrangement of "Jonathan Scrivener" and "Chaos is Come Again" is adhered to.[23]

*　　　*　　　*

Incidentally, how apt the fourth of the above quotations is in its application to the life of Fr[ederick] Rolfe. Perhaps it reveals the very heart of his life's mystery. The incident which recalled to me the name of Rolfe was the discovery amongst an immense heap of old magazines, a 1928 copy of "Life and Letters" containing an early article by Symons on Rolfe's life. But it proved to be a rather scamped and hurried assembly of the salient features of his career and gave no hint (except for one or two quotations from "Hadrian" and the letters, and a facsimile of his beautiful script), of the fascination of Rolfe's personality, the tragedy of his switchback care of fortune and the strange exotic preciosity of his medieval imagination.

*　　　*　　　*

These last three mails have brought no letters from Betty. I wonder why it is that the things one desires most seem to suffer the most hazards? Perhaps the poor darling is ill again, perhaps the letters have gone astray... I can imagine all kinds of possibilities except that she has not written. Her letters are my recurrent reason for maintaining my grasp on life. If they should ever stop for any reason that was decisive – I hesitate to name the shuddering consequence. Perhaps this fatal inertia, which I feel is not confined to me nor to this colony. Somehow the days slip away and nothing's done. All I can do is watch them in a kind of inert, remorseful stupor.

Last night I had a fine discussion with Packham on Shakespeare's severance from ordinary life. I maintained that Shakespeare's work had universal implications, that the stuff of human experience was a common inheritance with the human race. Packham thought his heroes bore no relation to and provided no insight into the emotions of the modern or even of the Elizabethan Tom, Dick and Harry. And I had the amazing good luck to convince him otherwise. Packham is one of those rare spirits who can be persuaded that he is wrong. Tho the admission usually cripples <u>any</u> argument.

*　　　　　*　　　　　*

Another mail without letters from Betty. I say, O Christ ...

Another mail without letters from Betty. I say, O Christ...

Last Echoes

Dust ebbing over dead cities
Leaves shuffling in crepuscular flocks
Before the vagrant herdsman winds
Leaves and dust and the silt of centuries
And rats scuffling over dead men's bones.
Dumb are the clocks in the crumbling pinnacles
And time is a mid-ocean calm.
No phantoms shift in the cobwebbed halls
And the last echo of the last laugh has dwindled
In the last silence of the end.
You historiographers probing
With aseptic pen in these derelict anatomies
Write not of the casual slaughter
Of big wars, of decadence and folly
Of mob-deaths and promiscuous ruin.
Reflect that here men laughed and wept
And filled mighty palaces with laughter and tears.
Here there was love great as Helen's or Antony's
Tender as Juliet's, sweet as Corydon's.
Old men died alone in the chill winters
Maidens were mourned when the blossoms were white.
Women bore children who in their joy
Decked streets with a confetti of cries
Wherever they played. Wise men
Foretold ruin and statesmen counselled.
Rodin and Epstein and Gill chiselled
Their visions and breathed life and the pain
Of Ages into inert stone.
Yeats wrote and Eliot, Shaw and Wells.
An obscure young man too
In a bare garret fed the tense flame
Of genius with his life and died,
Rich in poems in the anaesthesia
Of a gas oven. Gable touched
To passion the hearts of scullery-maids,
Jean Harlow died and Shirley Temple lived.
There were National and Derby where

The rivetter squandered shillings
And the ship-owner won thousands.
There were Dole and Dogs, and Darts
In the foetid camaraderie of Pubs.
There was Flu in Winter and making ends meet.
There was Hitler a Music-Hall joke
A preposterous posturing Chaplin
Then Hitler the Practical Joke
And young men in khaki leaving home
And No one cheering.
After that the bombs and shortly
Time was a casualty and there were
Intervals only between holocaust and holocaust
But there were jokes and there was laughter
In the time of the end.

Then a few men carousing
With some flotsam wine
In a leaky cellar and Each
Creeping away to the Privacy
Of His own Death...

IV

Rumours, Rumours
May 1941 to December 1941

On May 10, Scotland played host to one of the stranger episodes of the Second World War. Rudolf Hess, Hitler's second-in-command, in what appeared to have been an attempt to negotiate a peace settlement with Britain, parachuted into a field near Eaglesham, outside Glasgow, after flying solo across the North Sea in a Messerschmitt 110 from Augsburg airfield in Bavaria. He was apprehended by pitchfork wielding ploughman, David McLean, who, peering through the shadows, found a stranded Hess bound to the cold Scottish turf with a broken ankle, his true identity as Germany's deputy Fuhrer not apparent to McLean or others on the farm on which he worked.

"I was in the house and everyone else was in bed late at night when I heard the plane roaring overhead," McLean was quoted in the Daily Record. *"As I ran out to the back of the farm, I heard a crash, and saw the plane burst into flames in a field about 200 yards away. I was amazed and a bit frightened when I saw a parachute dropping slowly earthwards through the gathering darkness. Peering upwards I could see a man swinging from the harness. I immediately concluded it was a German airman baling out and raced back to the house for help. They were all asleep, however. I looked round hastily for some weapon, but could find nothing except a hayfork."[24]*

Whether Jack knew that the land of his birth had been catapulted into the headlines by such a hugely significant – if comic – event is unclear as he makes no mention of Hess' doomed flight. Neither does he make reference to the May 20 German airborne invasion of Crete nor to the sinking of the German battleship, Bismarck, *on May 27, which claimed the lives of 1,995 sailors out of a 2,200-strong crew. Instead, he concerned himself with the "deterioration of the situation in North Africa, Syria and Iraq" and that not insignificant global power, Russia. Having previously speculated over the Soviet Union's position in the conflict – and its then stance as a neutral state – Jack opted for the more sedate "The war* includes Russia" to register this monumental sea change in a world-wide struggle that was now almost two-years-old.

Russian military involvement began on June 22, 1941, when Soviet dictator Joseph Stalin was caught completely off-guard as German soldiers invaded the communist giant from the south and west, with a third force driving their way from the north towards Leningrad (now St Petersburg), trampling all over the terms of the non-aggression pact signed by both sides at the war's outset. Operation Barbarossa, as this audacious military assault was known, saw Nazi Germany make massive initial gains, taking what is today Belarus and vast swathes of Ukraine, and encircling Leningrad, with Soviet troops suffering some truly appalling losses. By the time Jack departed West African shores in December, however, Stalin's Red Army had driven back the Moscow-bound Germans – through the freeze of a cruel Russian winter – in what amounted to Hitler's first major defeat on land and what proved a significant blow to German military aspirations with the Fuhrer's designs of taking Moscow before the winter months having failed at enormous cost.

Here, two short stories, a written list of his reading material and a delivered speech to the debating society provide further evidence of Jack's strong inclination to work his grey matter in the face of his surroundings. Yet, against the backdrop of such global chaos and uncertainty – which also included the surprise Japanese attack on the American naval base at Pearl Harbor in Hawaii on December 7, 1941 (an act that drew the United States into the conflict) – 16 months wartime service in Freetown had left him with no little sense of frustration, even if he appeared to finally make peace with Britain's conduct in the war.

"From this tropical oasis we watched with an awful sense of impotence the wide slaughter which threatened our homes and our loved ones... but our country pulled thru and for that we have all the gratitude of anxious hearts for the R.A.F. whose strength and lack of weariness never faltered," he records as, no doubt buoyed by thoughts of his imminent return home, he brings his wartime memoirs to a rousing and patriotic close.

Inertia

Here in this tropic quiet where day
Bestrides green jungle and a huddled town
Love and hate pass in formless interplay
Of lost significance. We limply watch
Involved morrice of insects against the grey
Aspect of the past. Emotion has been bought
From this world. No one is gay
Enough to sing and no one wise enough
To know to whom to pray.
Here is but the multifoliate star
Of death and the remorseless sway
Of light and dark swinging on our sky.
All of us have somewhere lost the way
We sought. We have sat too long
In casual retreats until delay
Has poisoned our resolve. We turn
Now to the moonless night and bay
Our follies to Horizon's empty rim
Battening on the echo. We stay
And draw a sour and starveling sustenance
From alien dugs, a bitter lotos whey.
Idly we wait, waiting for nothing
Or hoping for Zarathustra to pass this way
And suddenly one become two.

Diary

I have omitted to date these entries. I never know the date and nobody seems able to enlighten me. At any rate it's somewhere around the beginning of May and three months – everybody says – from going home. They talk of educational classes for the men. My aid is enlisted. Personally I think it's a forlorn hope. The men are altogether too hard-worked and browned-off to take any active interest in such classes. And unless they are prepared to study privately, the lecturer is merely wasting his time. I suppose the authorities think it will prove a counter-attraction to the brothels. Considerable dubiety is permissible. AND –

Item: – There is a "bellum inferendum"[25]...

A certain "mental" patient admitted and boarded home by us in December of last year has just been taken off a ship in the bay, and brought up here! The orderly who took him home is still in England. The patient is being returned to the U.K. once more. Thus works the Army.

Seven dental officers without equipment have been idling at Accra for six months. Our D.O. was boarded home. All the work of the colony has devolved on Capt. Gollan, a D.O. unattached. But the Army has sent to England for another officer. (1) They could transfer Gollan to the 51st General. (2) They could supply an officer from the redundant staff at Accra. But no. They prefer the work to slide while they await replacements from England. My God!

$$*\qquad *\qquad *$$

Today a letter from Betty. Thank God she's well. Thank God for her love.

$$*\qquad *\qquad *$$

"'P-----' with Packham"

Another mail but from Betty – silence. Five mails and only one letter from her. I wonder where are all the letters she must have written between 1st and 15th April? This mail is a Gordian puzzle. Why should I worry, knowing she is well, having the assurance that her love is unabated? I don't know. But I do. The problem is an easy psychological one, but I'm not in a mood for self-analysis. And who would be, pray, after the nerve grinding of nine boring, debilitating, sick months in this tropical mausoleum? Nobody. Of course not.

Marrow weariness, subliminal hostility and the protean transmogrifications of fear for one's lover. Guck-gucking vortices of hate and shame. The sterile dawn of disillusionment; the vermilion blind of desire and the want deep in one's bowels. The stale bread of life and the quotidian formulae and the hopelessness of a conscious certainty. Matutinal bleakness, postprandial ennui, vespertinal drabness. Tomorrow, yesterday, today, next Monday. The arterial road of life. The unwelcome surety, this railway timetable life. Life is a cliché, a meaningless incantation in a wilderness, endless in repetition. O for the dank blast of T.S. Eliot. I cannot find one of his poems.

For the past month irritation cumulating has been finding its outlet in the hysterical exchange of insults. Packham's conversational penchant is to sustain a continuous barrage of insult and cruel wit. Sometimes Levy, "slimy-gutted b----d" with "a cash register mind"; sometimes Lees, sometimes Adams, sometimes myself he pillories. Tempers break often. Today I clouted him across the breakfast table and he returned the buffet. He has a knack of fraying one's temper, but he too often is tolerated. Anyway, I felt jangled and upset, hating myself for losing my senses, and loathing Packham for provoking me. I decided this morning he is just "a smart little Cockney with a cheap jazzy commercial mind". That is not a final estimate. I'm just piqued. And I like the blighter. But it is part of the truth all the same. I always had the idea that one gave things to one's friends, but Packham sells you everything. He sold me a nasty little belt for 1/- and a pair of mosquito boots for 10/-. Neither articles did he buy, but he made me pay for them. That I imagine is business. Thank heaven for the "professions".

"Cyril Packham trying to sell something to the village"

Packham pretends to be socialist. His own personality has been shaped by capitalism. An opportunist like he would never live in the uncompetitive moral atmosphere of a socialist utopia. But for all that he's stimulating as a friend, he has a refreshing freedom from respectable conventionalities. He's a sane, frank, hard-hitting little carthorse with ambitions of running in the Grand National, and a candid lack of scruples, material, moral, social, as to how he gets there. A life like that flourishes bay-tree-like, and suddenly pays evil dividends. But what life doesn't? Anyhow, I shall apologise and by lunchtime we'll be friends.

All this seems petulant. I wonder if it is? At any rate, it rationalises my emotions and I feel better having tried to be just to Packham and harsh with me. Tho I suspect I have merely put my tongue out at him, and patted myself soothingly on the head...

But if you want to discover your real opinion of your friends, quarrel with them.

But if you want to discover your real opinion of your friends, quarrel with them.

*   *   *

"No evidence can affect convictions which have been arrived at without evidence."

J.A. Froude (Essay on Dissolution of Monasteries)

*   *   *

There arrived a long letter from Betty, with a great deal of pleasant unaffected description of her visit to a farm in Lesmahagow. She suggests we visit the place together. I'd love to.

*   *   *

Griffin this morning – leave in September. God knows! The deterioration of the situation in North Africa, Syria and Iraq, the menacing proximity of Dakar and the constant raids we have from there by air, the massing of troops on the borders of Fr. Guinea (Griffin again!), these may make leave impossible for us. Then chaos is come again. Bush warfare is not the German cup of tea; bush warfare in the rains is not anybody's cup of tea. If we can get out before the dry season I think we'll be sure of our leave. Actually, if an attack by land is successful here, we are caught like rats in a trap. There are no docks to accommodate ships of sea-going size, and barges and tenders are pathetically few. Then, of course, we have 3,000 miles of sub-teeming ocean to navigate. Yes, we'd be in a tough spot. But nobody thinks about it. It's wiser not to.

*   *   *

"Heaven lies about us in our infancy and before we are very much older the world starts lying about us."
– Ambrose Bierce

*   *   *

Another mail today. Nothing from Betty. But a wonderful letter from Alistair Thompson. Blank verse in answer to my vers libre. Passages of keen incisive writing, balanced pertinent comment on the psychological front, ruthless self-examination and a very commendable candid detachment. All Alistair. A deal of good stuff. Relieved to discover the alopecia, which afflicted my attempt – the inevitable dropping of pitch, the occasional bathos, the prosaic parenthesis, the failure of verbal annotation to be sufficiently infused with meaning to make the impressionism successful. But there are some succinct phrases upon which the overtones and suggestions crowd, creating the suburban microcosm in one taut line.
The poems he appended do show improvement. His

Housman[26] attempt has the authentic note of bleak yet somehow minor tragedy, but is marred by an extra syllable in one or two places. The modern verse forms, I think, he does not accomplish near so well. There is an insufficiency of those "pep" phrases and a general lack of slickness in his presentation. Yet, again, the generalisation has the fault of all generalisation – by humorous definition it is usually false. And here and there, there are steely coruscations of real penetrative observation. In short, the entire letter was inexpressibly welcome and wholesomely nostalgic.

Letters from Betty dated 22nd and 25th April. Today is 1st June. I remember it because, as I am given to understand, I was precipitated into a world at war just 23 years ago today. The world is again at war. As the Archbishop of the Wasteland avers, "Here we go round the gooseberry bush," and the world ends "not with a bang but a whimper." Men were whimpering for a war-end at my nativity, today they're whimpering without object, out of sheer bewilderment, having just realised that tho princes make wars and they die in them, nobody is able to stop them. I read once a story of a farmer who bought a new traction engine. He got into the seat, pulled a couple of levers and the thing careered off over his corn, thru his hedges, demolishing a pig-sty and a hen-coop, and he stood up in the seat and wept to see his farm laid waste. There is a parallel there.

*   *   *

"Rabble in Arms". Pp. 196.

Doc Means – "Armies... armies was created special to encourage disease. You don't rest good in an army, and you're kind o' scairt most of the time; and when you ain't scairt, you're either mad or homesick. What's more, you're always too hot or too cold or too wet, and there's always some pitt-whistle of an officer making you do something disgusting, and your food's rotten, if so be you get any food at all; and all those things together fix

Pte/ Solomon A Bangali
25/7/41

Dear Sir

Words of Suitable terms are
not within my reach to express my sincere & hearty
wishes to you. Please Sir I am now asking you
kindly to do me this favour as you being my good
master. Sir, I Congratulate you most sincerely to
supply me with any of your old forage caps. I shall
be very happy and I will highly appreciate it. All my
mates are getting it gradually, but there is no one to
do me so. Should in case this my request be
granted, I shall endeavour to give you whatever
little I may get with all pleasure.

Awaiting to get your favourable
answer
Your in hoste:
Solomon

A letter to Jack from local Freetown boy Solomon asking for one of his "old forage caps", September 25, 1941 it so you can't help getting took sick. Then when you're sick those same things fix it so medicines don't do you no good, even when there <u>are</u> medicines, which there usually ain't. The way to cure these fellers of what ails them is to stop the war and send 'em home. There ain't hardly one of 'em but what would be healthy inside of a week."

*   *   *

I've been reading Galsworthy's "Flowering Wilderness". God, what an experience! Inside I feel exhilarated and bitter and exalted, confused, restless and intoxicated. Physically, I'm exhausted. The tragic drama of the love of Desert and Dinny is as great as anything Shakespeare conceived and I don't care who sees my confession. I never felt so spiritually battered in all my life as I do now after reading that book. And I'm scared to read anymore of Galsworthy's novels lest they should be less good.

If only Galsworthy had Shakespeare's poetry...

*   *   *

Virginia Woolf is dead. Suicide. The delicate instrument is the first to crack under the strain.

Virginia Woolf is dead. Suicide. The delicate instrument is the first to crack under the strain.

Hugh Walpole too is gone and "The Times" obituary follows him to the graveside with damnably faint praise. Alan Dent contributes a wonderfully sympathetic article in "John O'London's".[27]

With the going out of these two beautifully sensitive and rare spirits the world seems already smaller.

Soon my generation's links with the literary past will be snapped. Yeats has gone, and Davies, Virginia Woolf and Walpole. One day it will be G.B.S. and before long Priestley and the dramatic critics Agate and Prentis and

Morton. Then we ourselves will be tradition, we who have kicked and flouted and jeered at the traditional. What sort of figures will Huxley and Greene, Lewis, Auden, Dylan Thomas, Campbell and MacNeice, Dent and Williams cut with the mantles of authority upon them?

This age... you must label it, I think, "the age of scepticism." Yet when all beliefs are being subjected to the cold microscopic scrutiny of reason, when knowledge on all subjects is only a relative certainty, we are fighting a nation of our own age and civilization whose fanaticism over a creed of spurious ideals and scientific falsehoods has brought a horrible recrudescence of the Dark Ages on thousands of their fellow-citizens. It is hard to believe that the German people have really allowed this awful cataract to obscure their spiritual and mental vision. But now all that they share with us in common humanity they have forfeited because of a clique of megalomaniacs who have suborned them and inoculated their youth with all manner of evil. Because of the mental subjection and the blind fanaticism of its youth, a whole, great, talented nation is being branded as Huns and barbarians! But those who soil their lips with such denigration in public utterances are nothing more than demagogues and publicity-mongers. They inflame public opinion and reduce its already negligible detachment in forming views, when if ever a public needed to be cool-headed and sane and reasonable it is now. It is not so much the war as the peace, which must be won. A British victory may keep Britain secure for another quarter of a century, but a humane and just Peace will keep the world free from war perhaps forever! The first essential is a defeat for Nazi doctrines, of course, but we must not forget that we have an obligation to the world and generations unborn, for the future peace of Europe. If we fail then our victory will be dross, it will be a snare to take <u>our</u> sons into another more terrible holocaust. We cannot afford to mess up this peace. Beside the "V" for victory there should stand in letters of crimson – "R.P." – <u>remember the Peace</u>.

*   *   *

How it has rained this last week! Fierce, relentless rain falling from grey skies and then in the evening it stops and there are the stars flecking the electric-blue with gold. By day the earth lies sullen and livid under the ceaseless inoculation of those needles of rain. From the embankment great brown gouts of water leap as tho the very earth itself was bleeding fatally. It pounds on the tin roof like the drumming of a thousand fingers. Its force makes you want to strip off your clothes and feel it beating on your shoulders and cascading over your flanks in a magnificent contact with the elemental. A kind of flagellation I suppose...

But how it makes one long for the sunshine again. I suppose I shall be frozen to death when I go home. But what does it matter? To be with Betty again is something I dream about with my eyes closed. It hurts. These last few weeks it has been "bruited" that we must stay here for 18 months. Even the officers are of that opinion. Christ, how shall I ever tell Betty, poor dear, after having her hopes raised and expecting me so loyally in September? Goddam those frozen-faced, plaster-brained, doltish fools of leaders! Don't they understand? <u>Won't</u> they understand that when a unit has had to invalid home 15 men and has had to carry on without reinforcement an overcrowded hospital, that it is homicidal to keep them here any longer. Even the officers are becoming bolshie. We have 38 men in hospital this week, bad cases of malaria and dysentery all of them. Thirty-eight men out of about 90. Still the hospital is running. Still there is no question of leave. Those of us who are left are wondering whether we shall ever leave this place alive...

No cinemas, no amusements, every day another bed vacant in the barrack-room... God, it's intolerable. The C/O, it is reported, writes, "the morale of the men is excellent." The bread we eat is riddled with weevils and dead ants. Nauseating. The meat is tough and almost uneatable. A lab report on it mentioning indescribable bacteria. But we continue to eat it. There is nothing else.

The Padre, one or two of the M.Os are telling the men, "go in dock, go in dock, it's the only way to get reliefs, or force them to give you leave." Leave. A Joke.

But it worked, did that stratagem.

Five men and two officers were standing by to go on the SS Abosso. Suddenly came a cable cancelling it. "The Unit is being relieved." We were jubilant. Then joy gave way to caution and caution to suspicion. "Were we being duped?" None of us would be surprised. The question hangs fire for about 10 days.

Then –

You are being relieved in three parties, after 15 months, after 16-and-half, after 18. Good God! Done for. I'm sure to be on the last batch, sure to be. Last batch. Oh Hell!

But no. Amongst others, Adams, Packham, Levy and Rillie are going first. Relief.

We may go at the end of October or the beginning of November. But we are allowed to say only this to those at home. "Coming before Christmas." My poor Betty. She will think that ages. But I know it will be all the greater a surprise for her when I arrive earlier.

Tomorrow and tomorrow and tomorrow... indeed...

*　　　　　*　　　　　*

The war includes Russia. We make a stiff bow of friendship, and except for a 24-hour bombing of Germany, make little move to help. Can it be that after all we are still unprepared? God knows, but I'm sick to death of this war. And I suspect everyone but the red-tabs and the political orators is likewise. Of course we're caught in the avalanche now; it is easier to go on than go back.

Of course the point at issue now is not how we should have treated Germany. We've made blunders, ghastly ones, but in going to war to extirpate fascism we did not err. Granted, we did not make war soon enough or late enough – all that makes a painful passage in our history – but however inopportune our declaration of war I cannot doubt now the necessity or the rightness of it. Fascism in root and fruit, in idea and in manifestation is evil, an epidemic evil. It had to be destroyed. Incompetents with scrupulous pedigrees may mishandle our armies and waste needlessly, thousands of lives. Capitalists may batten on the war and profiteer and grow rich and fat. There may be gross inequality and tragic poverty and pitiful lines of unemployed after the war (there won't be if we are conscious). Yes, tho we may run thru the whole appalling cycle of 1918 onwards it will still be worth the poverty, the inequality, the futility, the waste....

But a wee small voice insists – yes, but not <u>your</u> poverty, <u>your</u> inequality, the making-futile of <u>your</u> life, the waste of <u>your</u> life.

Hush! you voice. I am being high-souled!

<u>Beautiful cable from Betty – the darling!</u>

26th July 1941 Remembering sadly and happily 26th July 1940 [28]

*   *   *

Major McComas opines we shall be lucky if we are home by the end of December... Fiddlesticks my dear Major, absolute poppycock...

*   *   *

Had a discussion last night on varietism and monogamy, I hitting out sturdily for monogamy. "Varietism is a symptom of dissatisfaction," I said, "dissatisfaction with life, discontent and restlessness due, in the last resort, to lack of self-knowledge. A person who indulges his lust and prostitutes his emotions will find them dulled in the end and the consequent lack of satisfaction in every relationship will compel him to be forever seeking a will o' the-wisp pleasure. The curse of Cain is upon him. On the other hand you will find that the person who is truly and deeply in love is instinctively monogamous. He or she knows that no kind of pleasure or satisfaction will derive from another relationship. It is not a painful moral self-discipline either, but a natural attitude which is unthinkingly maintained."

Said Willie, "But look here man – you assume that everyone is capable of loving deeply as you call it, and that we are all <u>able</u> to stick to one person within the legal contract of marriage. What happens when one of the parties to a union becomes fed-up and sick of his or her partner? That party seeks satisfaction elsewhere, or if he is too strongly bound by conventional respectability he continues to live with his wife (or the wife with her husband) and both are supremely miserable. No. The varietist, I think, has the best of both worlds. If he is foolish enough to marry and fails to be happy he has the training and temperament to look for happiness with someone else without hurting himself a great deal."

"Yes, Willie," I interrupted, "but far too many people marry for the wrong reasons. It is not an experiment in living for the consequences of failure are devastating emotionally and socially troublesome. Neither is it a guarantee of happiness. The parties to a marriage must not blind themselves to obvious difficulties, which may arise, nor must they be taken by surprise by irrational and un-looked for troubles. Each must be prepared to sacrifice himself or herself for the sake of the love, which binds them. That love must be preserved at all costs, for without it marriage will become a farce, a legalised prostitution, no matter how hard they try to make a success of it. There are very, very few vital things that should not be surrendered ungrudgingly to sustain love. And with the right attitude a couple will not ask of each other sacrifices which would involve serious bereavement and a consequent loss of good-feeling. But I've gone off the track – marriage is neither an experiment nor a guarantee. The varietist is not prepared to work for its success and if it fails him, as I think it probably will do, he chucks in the sponge and looks up another partner. He ought to be prepared to accept the fact that dilettantism in life as in art gives no spectacular results and provides no lasting happiness because it does not call for the whole exertion of one's being.

But the sting, I think, will be at the end when one is not so mobile and friends are fewer. Then becomes important the comfort of a woman with whom you have shared all the most intimate parts of life, a woman who knows and understands and forgives all one's faults and foibles, who has been with you in despair and in joy, and from whom nothing is hid in your life. I think at the last, in those remaining years when one is occupied only in waiting for death and in elaborating plans to forget it or stave it off, a wife will be the most precious happiness in the world."

"Mm. Maybe you're right," said Willie.

"Oh. I wish to heaven I were home and the war over".

"There," said Adams. "I'm with you every time."

*   *   *

In commemoration of our arrival in the colony a year ago to-day we held a "piss-up" complete with the funeral baked meats etc. Of course we had much of the brew that "puts a devil in men's mouths to steal away their brains." Everyone was scintillating with wit, but the morning after was grim and gloomy & I had most violent indigestion. Oo what a head!

*   *   *

August has gone. Today is September 6th. Levy has heard via the ADMS's barber (!) that we shall be <u>home</u> in two months. That leaves us about five weeks to wait for a boat and our relief. Heavens, I do hope he's right! If I arrive about the end of October, Betty won't be so disappointed after all. It is a bit late for her holiday. I've told her to take them as she arranged whether I am home or not. I don't think she will tho and I will be glad if she waits for me, tho if she does feel she needs them I really

<u>would</u> rather she take them earlier. But what a time we'll have at Kirn, or indeed anywhere. We shall be together anyhow and beside that nothing matters. I wish I could tell her I'm coming... but I can't.

Those green envelopes – a racket. By signing them you damn near sign your life away. The slightest slip and you're for court-martial. If the alternative weren't to allow our own "nosies" to read my letters I shouldn't use the darn things. But I'm out on a cleft stick. It's infuriating, this censorship. And with the officers (discovered and known to be the most impolitic of people) and sisters too censoring their own letters the whole business is a bloody farce.

O di immortales O pisces minimi![29]

The days drag their interminable length thru darkness and sunshine.

*   *   *

Lest we forget...

The following scintilla I caught and imprisoned here are from Castlerosse's "Love, life and laughter."

"There could be some brandy," he said, "that would make an impression on your stomach." He was quite right. It was like swallowing a torchlight procession.

"My God," she cried.

"Yes, madam," I replied, "but strictly incognito."

A flock of sheep, a gaggle of geese... a lamentation of virgins.

"Is this green thing a waistcoat?"

I said, "Yes, what did you think it was."

"A tennis-court," he replied.

*   *   *

20.00 hours. On Deck

I am alone. Alone. I can hear my pen scrabbling away at the words. Scrapings of a sharp pen in the silence. Then the screeching of a dry pen. That is all. In the end the futile screech of the dry pen. Outside there is the sea. But the monotony of its ceaseless lisp on the ship's side is a kind of silence. Sometimes it is a cheap and fawning whisper; the importuning whisper of harlotry. Then the silence is corroded with meanness. But mostly it is just there: a monotonous part of the silence. And I am alone and I can hear my pen telling you about it. When the ink is gone that is the end. At least as far as you are concerned. When the ink is done I am done. Perhaps it will go before I can say goodbye. And you will say he left without saying goodbye. I wonder what happened to him. And when the ink is gone dry I shall rise and creep away. My joints will be cold and I shall blow on my hands and push my chair back and rise and look at the sky and look at the sea. Then maybe I shall creep away, a young man in an old silence. The brilliant silence of the sky and the silence of the gnarled belly of the old sea are a symphony of silences. An atmosphere, an emotion, earth-old, familiar.

The sky. Semi lunar darknesses and shadows. Interstellar spaces, cold, distant, silent. Stars caught in a tangle of white hair, stars beautiful, stars aloof, stars silent. Death or lifelessness, perpetual soundlessness. They are the same; oblivion, silence, death.

And the waters. Flux continual. Change the only constant. The rhythm of the sub-sea life. Over the sea no wings beat. Only flux and reflux and the silence of the ceaseless whisper. In the quiet there is no life and only the monotone muted and part of the silence. And no spirit moves over the face of the waters...

A young man between the millstones of the old sky and the old sea. Twixt the silences a young man writing of old things. The scraping of a wet pen, then the creaking of a dry one. And that is the end. The final hieroglyph I am to you. And after that the silence and you say: I wonder what became of him.

The sky, the sea, a young man and a dry pen. And again the old silence...

My Reading out here has been -

Private Worlds	Phyllis Bottome
Now East, Now West	Susan Ertz
This Bed Thy Centre	Johnson
Studies in Shakespeare	Boas
Lawrence and the Arabs	R. Graves
Disraeli	Andre Maurois
Cranford	Mrs Gaskell
The Woman who Rode Away	D.H. Lawrence
Lady Chatterley's Lover	"
Rabble in Arms	K. Roberts
The Quest for Corvo	Symons
English Literature	Ifor Evans
The W Plan	Seton
The Dark Invader	Von Rintelen
Crime and Punishment	Dostoevsky
The Fountain	Charles Morgan
Portrait in a Mirror	"
My Name is Legion	"
Flowering Wilderness	John Galsworthy
Chekhov's Four Plays	Chekhov
Short Stories	Various Collections
The Daring Young Man	Saroyan
New Writing in Europe	J. Lehmann
Modern Poetry	Lynd's Anthology
	Kilham Roberts' Anthology
English Poetry	G.B. Harrison's Anthology
Romeo and Juliet	Shakespeare
Othello, Macbeth, Hamlet,	"
Twelfth Night, Julius Caesar,	"
Coriolanus, King Lear, Sonnets	"
Psychopathology of Everyday Life	Freud
Bases of Modern Science	Sullivan
Confessions and Impressions	Ethel Mannin
Green Willow	"
Sounding Brass	"

Crescendo	"
Children of the Earth	"
Clayhanger	Arnold Bennett
The Card	"
The Regent	"
Mr Polly	H.G. Wells
Kipps	"
Short History of Philosophy	C.E.M. Joad
The Story of Philosophy	Will Durant
Liberty and Representative Govt.	J.S. Mill
Love, Life and Laughter	Castlerosse
Wuthering Heights	Emily Bronte
Head in Green Bronze	H. Walpole
Let the People Sing	J.B. Priestley
Master of Ballantrae	R.L. Stevenson
As We Were	E.F. Benson
Froissart's Chronicles	Jean Froissart
Medieval People	E. Power
Ballet	A. Haskell
The Trimmed Lamp	O. Henry
Short Studies on Great Subjects	Froude
Annie Spragg	Bromfield
Joyful Delaneys	H. Walpole
Me	Naomi Jacob
Young Emmanuel	"
I am Jonathan Scrivener	Claude Houghton
Chaos is Come Again	"
A Novel of His Own Life	Gilbert Frankau
Mr Perrin and Mr Traill	H. Walpole
The Weather in the Streets	R. Lehmann
It's a Battlefield	G. Greene
Brighton Rock	"
Devil Rides Out	D. Wheatley
Those Were the Days	O. Sitwell
Stalky and Co.	R. Kipling
How Like an Angel	A.G. Macdonell
The Great Victorians Vols. I and II	Various Authors
Antic Hay	A. Huxley
Hind Let Loose	C.E. Montague

A five-minute speech made in our Current Affairs 90-minute session:

Subject was, "Is democracy an adequate form of Government under any circumstances." I was briefed as "Advocatus Diaboli" along with Rt. Hon. Packham and Mr Justice Adams. Here is my contribution.

"Mr Chairman, Gentlemen,

You have heard the argument in defence propounded by the last speaker. I am sure that none of you doubt his integrity nor his sincerity. Indeed, when it comes to sincerity one can only stand afar off and wonder. Was there ever such an eloquent plea since Baldwin wept rhetorical tears over England, His England? But we must not, must we, be cynical about such a beautiful faith as is our Honourable Friend's. We too must be sincere; we too must have faith in God and Democracy and for all Britons a celestial Isle of Man after death. But non nobis Domine, not unto us, O Lord was given that faith which can remove mountains by not thinking about them. And tho I speak not with the tongues of men and of Angels I have charity and I forgive myself freely for the temerity, which allows me to jitterbug (if I may so speak) in the very pantheon of this gentleman's life.

Democracy, we are asked to believe, is the acme of social achievement? And it is not to be wondered at either that it has been nurtured and brought to blossom by the British nation? How regrettable that mine should be the discordant voice in all this (hypothetical) unison of acclamation! I accept my task with the shrunken timidity of the man who coughed in one of H.M. Bateman's cartoons. But a kind of perverted Jiminy Cricket urges me to extravagances of irreverence and orgies of desecration.

We have, in that land of Blessed Memory, Gt. Britain, a government described by its members, adherents and obliging electorate as Democratic. Every man over the age of 21 is assumed to carry a Prime Ministers Cigar in his waistcoat pocket. Such is the measure of our thoroughness in equalitarianism. Moreover, the people may, if they so choose, elect to govern them such personalities as Stan Matthews or Gracie Fields or George Formby. But they invariably prefer people of whom they know infinitely less, strangers who call at their homes once in a hectic electioneering month and smile beautifully and make wondrous promises and then disappear for five years into the dim limbo of Westminster. It is indeed passing strange.

But it is not my province to criticise the axe-grinders who compete in these travestied polling booths. I trespass if I mention the odd paralysis, the petrifaction which afflicts those men who returned to Westminster big with promises.

The catchphrase of democracy, the central pillar of its existence, "All men are equal". Let us consider that, for on it rests the whole edifice. All men are equal in law therefore they are equal in all respects. For a moment one might suppose we were considering the Euclidean plane figure but we are not. It is the loose unconformable human organism, the unpredictable, dissimilar vagaries of the human nature.

Yet this tenet is on the lips of every canting politician, in the lines of every wash-leather sentimental versifier, in the crude prolegomena of every revolution and every war. It is stated without reservation. It is balm to the poor to reflect that they are "equals" of the rich; it gives the rich a warm inner glow of humanity to confess their kinship with the poor. The dolts and dullards and moronic nincompoops hail the dictum with howls of joy. The pseudo-intellectuals smarm it over with a comfortable patina of half-baked philosophy. Equal in law, equal in all respects. What sophistry! What preposterous balderdash! Drivelling nonsense dressed in a tailor-made format of logic. And it is this delusion, which is responsible for the blundering bungling myopia of soi-disant democratic governments.

The evil is implicit in any democratic constitution. The equality of men is an absurdity, a delusive lucubration. I put it to you. No one uneducated in art is competent to judge the merits of a picture. No one who is not a physician is equipped to diagnose the nature, origin and cure of disease. Is the dustman in matters of art the equal of the artist or the plumber in matters of disease the equal of the physician? When the Royal Academy requires a President ought it to appeal to the people to elect the man of their choice? When a clinic requires a chief ought the post to be given to the most eloquent vote-catcher, the idol of the people?

I ask you to follow me one step further down this stairway of glib inanity. Is the man who has no knowledge of politics, no knowledge of economics, no knowledge of dialectical intricacy competent to judge the truth or error of a treatise, which is a compost of politics, economics and dialectical nicety? Is such a man able to discriminate between the plausible theories of the vote-chaser and the recondite dissertation of the scholar? Is such a man able to discriminate between chicanery and sincerity, between logic and sophistry, between mere plausibility and absolute truth in matters of which he has no knowledge? I insist that such a man will be influenced, not by the reasonableness of any argument, not by cool ratiocination, but by the winning personality, class allegiance to a party, by emotional appeal. In other words by the wrong factors.

Is it not true that the majority of men have had no guidance or training in logic, and no knowledge of politics? Moreover, it is true that a mob or mass is susceptible to tides of opinion, which do not affect the solitary individual. And it is agreed that these waves of emotion, these clamant prejudices, are not conducive but inimical to clear thinking, that in fact they invariably lead to wrong courses of action. There is a Latin tag, "Vox populi vox Dei."[30] Rather I would say, Vox Populi vox suidei.[31] The Voice of the People is the voice of its God, its simulacrum. The Voice of the People is but a monstrous and distorted echo of the voice of its demagogue or its Fuhrer, its Duce or its President. Its voice is admirably suited to the conflicts of the arenas of boxing and football, but in the forum of politics where cool heads and wise counsels are vital, it is discordant, incongruous, above all it is lethal to wisdom.

The indictment of democracy does not end here, but I have said enough to imperil at least its claim to logicality. Democracy makes every Tom, Dick and Harry eligible to rule and judge policy. It neither requires that the elected have the seal and guarantee of expert knowledge nor that those who elect should have the most infinitesimal moiety of political learning.

A democratic government is in fact a glib and eloquent pack of mediocrities and hoodlums elected by a horde of apathetic incompetents and ignoramuses.

It is neither my duty nor my intention here to offer you political alternatives and social panaceas. The criminalism, the enslavement, the whole disgusting edifice of a government erected on murder and maintained by thuggery, which is the Fascism of Germany, I loathe and hate. Communism, with its fanatical loyalty to one class, its lust for uniformity and hatred of individualism, I reject. Human society is a growth in time not a syllogism in logic. It is an organism, not an organisation. You cannot pour society into the straitjacket of any Utopia. Democracy is a disastrous failure, Communism is a reflex of Capitalist evil, and Fascism is the most monstrous dangerous autocracy of vice, which has ever soiled the face of Europe.

I can only make one suggestion for our country and for the world. The strategical manoeuvring of parties and nationalities for power and the spoils of domination must give place to the rule of the best men, the exercise of statesmanship, which is the coordination of social forces and the adjustment of policy to growth.

There is no other exit from this sordid bewildering maze of miserable intrigues, uneasy truces and the horrible mass-murder of WAR.

Adapt our Plato to modern needs. Raise an aristocracy of brains. Let Wisdom and Sanity and Sincerity go hand in hand with deliberation, administration, execution. We must turn our backs on self-flattering concepts, relinquish our right to be consistently and dangerously misled and entrust to informed and enlightened men the government of the world."

Death of a Soldier

I watch him die. I sit on my pack by his side and with my hands on my knees watch him. With my eyes I have traced every lineament of his fading countenance. The dark hair is matted and limp. The roots of hair bordering his brow are seeded with tiny globules of perspiration and the dampness seeps through his forehead and lies in the furrows of suffering. His thin eyebrows are arched in linear bewilderment. The eyes swing restlessly under the pale integument, darkly they are shadowed behind closed lids. They are pebbles in the depths of a shaded pool. The face is cut into many planes of emaciation; the upper denture having been removed he breathes stertorously through sagging lips. The long thin fingers with the bitten nails weed restlessly the coat I have thrown over him. I think before evening he will be dead.

I hope he will die while it is still light enough to see to dig. I would not start before he dies.

We are in the stippled shadow of a great tree. The grey smooth column of its trunk is cool and pleasant to touch. Its leaves are broad and clean like a spread hand. The trunk is calm but the boughs are tortured into writhing forms as if there were a madness within. The leaves hang motionless in the heat. A sour miasma wreathes over the swamp and the air is rank with the odours of decomposition. The grimness here is an intoxication, a febrile luxuriance. A fat old bird puffs its feathers and regards us from a tree. It is noon. Everything waits.

And I await his death. Yesterday he was jealously hoarding his life, now he is weakly spendthrift. In the night I heard him whimper and I put my hand out to him and he was silent like a child. In the beginning he would talk, explaining endlessly, now fearfully, now defiantly, how he had to leave Corporal McGlade to the Japs. They tied him to a tree and bayoneted him six times. And Rex McGlade was my friend. But that is all over now. And the man who left him there is dying now at my feet.

We inhabit different worlds now. He has left me to

remember things alone while he busies himself with fantasy. I am his mother, his wife and his child all by turns. I am more than them all together for he looks only to me for succour. I see him with fear in his eyes when the fever is at its height. I say, "You will live Macfarlane". And it quiets him because I say so. He believes me and for a moment I feel pity for him.

Yesterday he said to me, "You don't like me" and I told him for Christ's sake to quit jawing. But it is true. The narrow eyes whose pigment is fading, the pinched nostrils, wet drooping underlip, the voice meagre and nails bitten to the quick. I know nothing of him. Time has cast us up and drifted out again. Sometimes in the distance I hear the guns but they are the rumour of an old quarrel we would forget. He has already forgotten. And we are together involved in his death. He knows and at first it strengthened his will. Now he looks at me as if I were his betrayer. He turns his head and opens his eyes and I see sight quickening in them as the wind stirs a furred ember to a glow. I see it in his eyes, hot, sharpened, driving into me. I blunt his gaze and it turns to fear and he speaks again. "Don't go away". I am smeared by his humiliating dependence and turn my eyes away. "Sleep," I say.

And he sleeps. His breathing is fast and shallow, tremulous like an animal's. When I slip my hand into his tunic pocket and remove his paybook he does not stir.

83430219 Macfarlane, William Albert. Trade. Date of Birth. All the details. Identification marks. Scar below left knee. Tattoo on right forearm. A heart pierced by an arrow. "Beryl" in red. Beryl living at Chapeltown, Leeds. A dingy brick house in a long terrace of broken railings and blackened gardens, grey sleeves of fog covering the bare trees. He is dying and she does not know. After many months a dry official note of regret from a grateful government, through the rusty letterbox on a dark morning. Our Albert killed. The dull bewildered grief of it. And then the slow forgetting, the getting used to the lonely bed. The kid will never remember its father. He will say he was killed in the war. Killed in the war, he will tell his friends, reciting the phrase he has been told. They will know nothing of me who sat watching him die nor of the man he betrayed.

My head aches, long fingers of pain spreading up the back of my head, hot probing roots driving down into my brain. I kneel down by the pool. A bright green snake rustles quickly from the reeds, an emerald tongue of flame darting into the undergrowth. I push aside the scum from the water, piling it neatly like a coverlet in a small semi-circle. I bathe my face, splashing the water on my throat and over the back of my neck, feeling the cold trickles run over my chest and down my spine. I thrust my hands down into its darkness and feel its coolness like bracelets on my wrists. Then I unwind the dressing on my leg. The blackness spreads in a dark stain from ankle to knee and the wound gapes like a mouth filled with pus, the lips dry and crusted. I know the signs, that blackness. One leg and a tortured bluish stump. I laugh. I throw my head back and laugh till my head rings and my belly-muscles ache. Then quite suddenly I am sick. I turn to see if the noise has awakened Macfarlane. His feet twitch. So, an unconscionable time a-dying, gentlemen. The freakish memory makes me smile. We have so much time to spare.

I soak the bandage and cover the wound. Then I rise and walk carefully to his side. I stretch myself on the warm earth.

I wake and my hands behind my head are numb. There is an awakening in the bush all around us. Rustlings, and scratchings and hoarse calls and vivid screams. The shadow of the tree lies in a deep pathway athwart our bodies. A restless clicking of tongues issues from the underbrush.

I know before I look at him that he is dead. I sit before him on my pack and with my elbows on my knees clasp and unclasp my hands. While he is there I am not alone. All around me there is life breathing and pulsating and quivering, life in the sleek movement, in the nimble run, and silent arrested pause. And there is this man beside me, a dank, spent wind in the shadows, this man whom I don't know is dead.

Now the time has come to dig. Soon it will be dark. I sit here clasping and unclasping my hands and waiting for him to open his eyes and curse me.

Dead, dead for a ducat. Lug the guts. No flowers. The vultures hang in sinister hieroglyph above the clearing. Remorseless wake.

With my entrenching tool I begin to dig. Neatly as I have been taught. The tool bites, the earth flakes away. My clothes are soaked in sweat and my head aches abominably. Pain drives through my leg with the relentless rhythm of piston strokes. I pause in my work to let the pounding abate. And suddenly I am cold. My body is shaken as if by the teeth of some ferocious animal. My muscles and all the tissues of my body contend in a great struggle and I watch, a fearful spectator, with my mind. Then the vortices of pain become shallower until they are only concentric ripples widening gently from a central focus. The cacophony recedes into the darkness that is closing, closing all around in great shrouds, cutting down the pillars of sunlight in swathes. It is as if I looked through the wrong end of a telescope, everything diminishes and fades. Darkness spreads its wings.

I wake to the sound of my own laughter. I cannot stop. It roars and peals and returns to me. My laughter returns to me a stranger. And then I stop. My stomach crawls in recurrent waves of nausea. I retch and spit the vomit onto the broken earth. Every part of my body tingles with drying perspiration.

It is darker, the brief dusk before nightfall. The cicadas shuttle madly, intently. It is still there, the stiff. I have still a job to do.

Whole days and nights, telescoped into one another and extended to infinity, pass as I struggle to roll the corpse into the shallow grave. It is night and starlit before I have shovelled the earth over and all is concealed. The cross and the discs, to mark the Christian and identify the soldier.

All is finished. And I lie down on the earth still warm from the body of the man I have buried. Above me in the high branches, silhouettes of menacing shadow stir against the sky. As I fall again into sleep, they stir fatly and settle in dark attitudes of expectancy.

15th December 1941

And now on the eve of homegoing what correspondence between the sum of things in their imaginative context and as they were in actuality.

This diary has been a barometer reflecting the falling and rising pressure of circumstances. It has been a kind of pool-mirror reflecting the heavens, distorting sometimes, misleading often as to the realities that lay behind the ruffled surface and the angry heavens it seemed to reflect. There is anger, unreasonable anger; wild illogical fits of pique: un-understanding conclusions especially about the conduct of the war. But it was all catharsis. There were dark days for us out here when our country faced invasion and took blow after blow on her strained and wounded flanks. From this tropical oasis we watched with an awful sense of impotence the wide slaughter, which threatened our homes and our loved ones. It did not make pretty watching. But our country pulled thru and for that we have all the gratitude of anxious hearts for the R.A.F. whose strength and lack of weariness never faltered. Only those who watched can know how much their prowess meant to us out here. We could do nothing but pray for courage and strength for those fighter pilots.

'And now that is over. We are hitting back. Only the competence of our chiefs could have carried our country thru that twilight drubbing & shows us not mere survival but Victory.

And now that is over. We are hitting back. Only the competence of our chiefs could have carried our country thru that twilight drubbing and show us not mere survival but Victory.

We've done our job: we're going home. For me, Betty, for six wonderful weeks, and then I shall be back again, where, whither, who knows... We operate each one of us ordinary soldiers a greater purpose than we know.

After securing a War Degree, Jack poses for his graduation photograph at the University of Glasgow, April 18, 1942

There is a Splendour of Light

"We must have a cause for whose sake we are all dear to one another" –
Nietzsche

Go. There is a splendour of light
You will see beyond the last ridge.
Take hands man, grip hands and go
Secure the morning within precious bands
Stronger than minister's asseverations
Not weaker than love. Look man now
On all new things, hearken the new voices
Of the old yearning world. Break open
The casks of your pity and yield
To the unarmed Christ.
O there is the salient you sought
In the harsh years of your fighting
In the bitter Autumns of your innocence,
Not overcome with flowers but
There is earth there, fecund enough
And sweet. See the translucent dawn
Opening beyond you and the green wind
Stirring and the cold stars dying, dying.
Come. Here graven in these pitted hands
Is the charter of our needs, the holy worth
Of love. Men will move to meet
The honest statement of your eyes,
Will match your faith with theirs.
This is peace. To hear the wanderer
Calling and to hail him. To set a light
To draw timid wings out of darkness
And not destroy. It is peace to wear
Upon your back a world's scars
And on your heart its care. Peace
Wears not the conqueror's mien.
Defeat is indivisible and there is no escape
Across the neutral frontiers of insouciance,
Its bitter ruined mouth speaks only
The broken syllables of new disaster.
Fare forth with your enemy and chart
The unmapped country of his heart
This is the hour to break down nonchalance,
To raise the spires of our sovereign pity
And forge new bells to call a world
To meet the promise of this morning's angelus.

For the West African Force

There is no sleep nor rest,
No bending of the will
For those who trembling fill
The ranks which held the best.

For this toil they were born
Comrades of the dead!
To let the blood flow red
And stain the ripening corn.

No bastion but their flesh
Thwarts the streaming tide
But others that have died
Preserve their courage fresh.

Here in this tropic quiet
Where no guns speak
Nor iron sirens break
The sleeping mercy of the night,
We do not fail
Those who die beside
Sour bomb-craters, who ride
Dark winds to sow avenging hail
With those who bleed
On Libyan sands, with those
On blood-starred Moscow snows
We serve a need.

Epilogue

"C'mon all you Jocks! We're in the bloody Clyde!"

Such words, as shouted on deck of their outbound ship from Freetown, and recalled by Jack in the written reminiscences of his life – which he penned many decades later – must have summoned the sort of elation he once thought lost during his long spell in Sierra Leone.

"On deck, on the port side, through the mist, we could just make out the endearing little lump that was Ailsa Craig," he recollected. "It took ages after that for the slowing ship to get as far as the Cloch. One began to see Dunoon, Kirn, the Holy Loch. We were ferried then from the ship, and unloaded onto Gourock Pier."

Having survived so many unpredictable days and nights in a far-off British colony, which, for better or worse, he now knew intimately, he returned to Scotland to find Betty newly ensconced at the Ministry of Information, and occupying a flat looking out onto Glasgow's Botanic Gardens. War was still raging, however, and Jack's work was far from done. In February 1942, he was posted to Horley in Surrey – "I can't think what Horley was for," he wrote – then Penshurst in Kent where he became a wardmaster in what he described as a "late Victorian institution in spacious grounds" dealing with skin infections. Here, he talked of "men mooching around with blue or green faces and/or hands. A lot of scabies, crabs, a variety of venereal infections. Scales of skin in some corridors – odours of unknown origin."

Reunited with his friend Cyril Packham and others he met in Freetown, Jack's time in Penshurst seems to have provided some welcome relief to his gruelling posting in Sierra Leone. Betty visited for weekends, there were quizzes, spelling bees, concerts and a "busy and eminently sociable" pub on the River Medway in which he enjoyed pints of mild and bitter from large barrels on the counter. On April 18, 1942, Jack reluctantly accepted a so-called War Degree – a "kind of bargain basement offer" – from Glasgow University, which, established in the summer of 1940 by Scottish universities, was granted to undergraduates who had completed just two years of study at a university, as well as a period of military service.

By 1944, Jack found himself in Catterick, North Yorkshire, and awaiting the birth of his first child – my mother. Judith Anne Marena Rillie was born

Jack in Kumasi, Gold Coast, July 1945, front row, second left

Jack in Accra, Gold Coast, c.1944-45, extreme right

on March 4, 1944, just days before Jack was due to leave the shores of Scotland and Britain once more. Indeed, after spending embarkation leave with both Judy and Betty in Glasgow, West Africa's vast deepwater frontiers loomed with a weary familiarity. But, this time it was not Sierra Leone that awaited the now 25-year-old father-of-one, but the Gold Coast, a British colony on West Africa's Gulf of Guinea, just a few degrees north of the Equator.

As opposed to Sierra Leone, Jack did not keep a diary of his time in the Gold Coast, even if he did compose some more West African-inspired war poetry. Essentially, all that remains of his 20 months in what is now modern-day Ghana are the retrospective notes he made as an octogenarian. In any case, after departing the British Isles in another lone Armed Merchant Cruiser, he ended up in Kumasi – "a well laid-out town with space" some 155 miles northwest of the capital Accra and accessed via the colonial railway – which was "equipped for civilized life and business and featured a bank, post-office, recognisable shops (often run by Lebanese) and a fairly decent hotel, which, as well as a dinner menu, had a band on Friday and Saturday nights."

Here, he was drafted into what he termed the Gold Coast Recruiting Organisation whose remit was to comb the Northern Territory for new recruits from outlying villages. As part of this very colonial job-description, Jack met with the respective local headman, drank local beer, "handed-round in large basins", and inspected potential new blood with suspect ages, many of whom carried umbilical hernias. Indeed, as a member of the RAMC, Jack was most intrigued by the various illnesses that plagued the locality as he later noted.

"On a visit to a leper colony, I once attended the amputation of an enormous breast (elephantiasis) – the patient out with drops of chloroform on a pad over her face, a native orderly with a large pail catching the breast as it fell!"

He also came into contact with the notorious trypanosomiasis (or sleeping sickness) and schistosomiasis (or bilharzia), a parasitic disease, which, affecting the urinary tract and intestine, was often the subject of his many war stories.

"When we visited the villages, we would ask the tribal elders if anyone pissed blood," he would say, a trademark twinkle in his eye, his posh west-end accent smoothing the story's ever so rough edges.

"'Here, everyone piss blood!'" came the retort (and punchline to an oft-repeated anecdote during many a family gathering).

Second World War Kumasi

*A woman of the B'Moba
ethnic group in Gambaga
(today's Northern Ghana),
c.1944-45*

Jack, who suffered only a minor attack of rubella during his long tour of duty in the Gold Coast, returned to Scotland in November 1945 and, with the war now over and comprehensively won by the Allies, de-mobbed with the rank of sergeant, for which he cared little. Not content with his War Degree, however, he re-enrolled at classes at Glasgow University in October 1946 and graduated with a first-class honours degree in English Language and English Literature in June 1948. This was to be his ticket to not only the world of paid employment, but a lifelong career with the scholarly recognition he so craved. For barely had the ink dried on his amended certificate, that he was offered the position of "Assistant in English" at Glasgow University for the modest starting salary of £450. And, there he stayed, rising through the ranks – and pay grades – and eventually making head of department.

Glasgow, where his second daughter, Jacqueline, was born in 1950, became his life, as did the university itself, where, with the likes of the late Scots Makar, Edwin Morgan, he made some of his closest friends, and taught and influenced several generations of students, who – Morgan wrote in Thirteen Ways of Looking at Rillie – would readily "testify to his brilliant but never pedantic qualities".[32] Yet, despite his career taking him to some of Britain's most ancient seats of learning, he never again left the shores of the United Kingdom (barring one trip to Dublin), his years in West Africa having somewhat jaded, as far as overseas travel was concerned, his ever-curious mind.

In 1962, Jack—who, with his penchant for snappy bow-ties, was fondly described as "... a dapperly dressed man, with a hit of a young Einstein about the head,"[33] by former student-turned writer, William McIlvanney — bought a large late Victorian mid-terrace villa in Glasgow's plum Broomhill district, which, featuring his much-prized study with its wall-to-wall books, stacked papers and large bay-window, he shared with his family and where he himself lived out the rest of his days. Betty's death in September 2004 was a loss from which Jack never fully recovered. He died of natural causes in November 2009 at the age of 91, his love of the written word and his compulsion for keeping copious amounts of notes, scribbling almost anything and everything that fired his literary-fuelled imagination, surviving to the very last.

"Now it is over...."

Now it is over, I remember
Tuneless things, a fractured sentence,
Words a tide has strewn, the song
Winds make in the hollow bone.
I think of the night barrage
And the buffet of saffron flame,
The crucial jest when the air
Was pungent with fear.
And the single anonymous voice
Of the dying.

Now as I walk the long streets of peace
Where the old no longer welcomes
And the familiar is ghostly of the trodden way
Unwontedly galls the feet
I think of men who yielded compassion
In full measure, now all dispersed, or dead.
And men of my generation in cities
Wandering alone, learning to walk again,
To use glib counterfeits for love & kindliness
And many would be glad enough to be,
With friends, afraid again.

Now it is Over

Now it is over, I remember
Tuneless things, a fractured sentence,
Words a tide has strewn, the song
Winds make in the hollow bone.
I think of the night barrage
And the buffet of saffron flame,
The crucial jest when the air
Was pungent with fear.
And the single anonymous voice
Of the dying.

Now as I walk the long streets of peace
Where the old no longer welcomes
And the familiar is ghostly and the trodden way
Unwontedly galls the feet
I think of men who yielded compassion
In full measure, now all dispersed, or dead.
And men of my generation in cities
Wandering alone, learning to walk again,
To use glib counterfeits for love and kindliness
And many would be glad enough to be,
With friends, afraid again.

Jack holding court at his beloved University of Glasgow, c.1975

Afterword

Students of literature in Peter Alexander's Glasgow University English department were lucky in their mentors. Professor Alexander (Regius Professor of English Language and Literature from 1935 to 1963) had an edition of Shakespeare to his name. John Bryce walked with Milton, had clearly read everything and made literary theory addictive. Sean Purser and Hannah Buchan were Wordsworthian though it was rumoured that Mr Purser would have preferred a career in football. Charles Salter was iconography and Augustans. Kilted Tom Livingstone gave the impression he had just come from a chat with Tennyson and Philip Drew, being Dickensian, was thereby omniscient, like the other Shakespearean, Ernst Honigmann, whose youthful appearance couldn't disguise formidable scholarship.

Jack Rillie and Edwin Morgan shared an office. They were the Moderns, the now men, from T.S. Eliot to the Beat generation. We called them "The Rillie-Morgan Axis". They were hip. Intimate with existentialism, Samuel Beckett and the writings of angry young men. A whiff of sulphur on Gilmorehill. A cell.

Some called him "Flash Jack". Others, mainly lady denizens of the extra-mural classes in which he took literature to hundreds whose trades and professions left time for such pursuits only in the evening, chose to see in the hair, the moustache and bow tie a Robert Louis Stevenson clone. Later he evolved into a blend of Einstein and Toscanini and we called him "The Sage". Whatever you called him, however you saw him, what you heard was incomparable. Ignition the second he stood at the lectern, cleared his throat of the last cigarette and raised a hand in greeting, palm almost upward as if to say, "See what I'm bringing for you". As if to say, "Come on, let's look at this together". And so we looked and listened while, ever Eliotesque, he came from the deep space of tradition with his show of individual talents. If this was Eng. Lit. it was also news of life and we couldn't get enough of it. But where did it come from, this grace beyond mere intelligence and learning? He professed what he so evidently loved and loved what he professed, this Windhover man in his dappled sports jacket mastering the air of the English classroom.

You were sure he was bringing us the news not just from his affairs of the mind with the writers it was our business to study but from a wider *engagement, profoundly human. We didn't know about his War, time out in Sierra Leone, but surely he had to be earthed. And earthed he was, as we found out, in his wife, Betty, and daughters, Judy and Jacquie and then in their marriages and his grandchildren as his earth expanded. His other element was water, especially the River Endrick and while he happily angled for its brown trout he also spoke out for their rights against the menaces of pollution, acid rain and the fashionable corporate bullying that favoured salmon and sea trout. Fashion wasn't much cop with Jack though he was less scathing than Thoreau. The bow tie added dash, but it was really as amiably archaic as his blessed repudiation of critical jargon.*

In the mid-sixties he became a colleague. How lucky could a former student get? This was true graduation, and the next instalment in a lifelong debt of gratitude. A bonus was the shared enjoyment of American literature, which developed into a determination to bring it into the curriculum. Much preparation was required. What would the books be? How would we link them into a story of the American grain and what distinguished American from English literature? So we began to plan, which meant we talked often and long. The Rillie sitting room was requisitioned for our weekly brainstorm and in came the big guns of the American Renaissance for us to argue about. We usually got into our stride about 8 pm with Emerson's transparent eyeball, Thoreau's frogs and mice, whippoorwills and pumpkins, Hawthorne's power of blackness and the whiteness of Melville's grand hooded phantom. Before things got completely out of hand Betty would come in about ten o'clock dispensing coffee, ham rolls and reality before leaving the boys to their barbaric yawps. A selection of Emily Dickinson's loaded miniatures would be, in Sir Thomas Browne's phrase, "the dormative we took to bedward". As often as not that was three in the morning and we were both stoned on ideas, language and camaraderie. It was a lovely life on that raft with Jack, "free and easy and comfortable".

When Betty died after ten months of steady decline, oh the difference to Jack. Now the crying inside throughout her illness could come out and he could mourn with all the others bereaved of mother, grandmother, friend. He could speak about the house in Rowallan Gardens full of everything Betty made, chose, arranged, loved, touched which was now a house full of detailed absences, an emptiness which crept into the sense of self. Writing about this a few years ago he said, "One does not crave more and more life at 89". Vexed and saddened by the feeling that he was now pulling away from the world, we took a while to realise that

162

even in his extremity he was still on his game. What he wrote about loss and loneliness in the empty house came from the same impulse to tell what he saw in his beloved Hopkins, Eliot and Wallace Stevens. He was annotating the margins of the poem, probing the text for the words that would suffice.

We all know that only part of the meaning of a poem can be conveyed by paraphrase. Nor can we paraphrase the life of a man, especially when the man has been himself a poem. Paraphrase takes us to a frontier beyond which words fail, though meanings still exist. That's how it is with the life of Jack Rillie. So here is the frontier from which we look towards meanings past the power of words; but surely we can see that the key to Jack's meanings is love.

Marshall Walker
Hamilton, New Zealand
June, 2014

Jack reading Thirteen Ways of Looking at Rillie, *Clarence Court, Glasgow, 2004*

Notes and References

1 – Graham Greene, The Heart of the Matter (Penguin Books, 1962; first published by William Heinemann, 1948), P. 115

2 – The Peace Pledge Movement was officially known as the Peace Pledge Union, a pacifist group that was formed by Dick Sheppard in the 1930s

3 – "Directive No. 16; On the Preparation of a Landing Operation against England", July 16, 1940

4 – "Te Vermiculum Laudamus" translates as "We praise thee, O worm", a parody of the well-known psalm, "Te Deum laudamus" – "We praise thee, O God"

5 – Graham Greene, Journey Without Maps (Vintage, 2006; first published by William Heinemann, 1936), P. 30/31

6 – ibid, P. 26

7 – ibid, P. 25

8 – ibid, P. 26

9 – ibid, P. 26

10 – An extract from Shakespeare's King Lear

11 – King Tom is an area of Freetown. The King Tom Cemetery contains 248 Commonwealth burials of the Second World War, and 129 burials of the First World War

12 – In the Homeric poems Death is called the twin "brother of Sleep"

13 – An extract from William Wordsworth's Ode: Intimations of Immortality from Recollections of Early Childhood

14 – Tamba was one of the native men responsible for Jack's general care

15 – Jack may have been less than impressed with Lt. Col. J.P. McGreehin, but he was perhaps unaware that McGreehin had won the Military Cross in the First World War. His citation recorded his 1918 heroics as follows: "While proceeding to assembly positions he was knocked over by a large piece of shell and badly shaken. Nevertheless, he pushed on and established his O.P. behind a bank. Unfortunately, unknown to him, it was in the vicinity of a water point, and was very accurately shelled all day and finally hit. In spite of this he worked on with the greatest courage, dressing with care all the wounded, and in one case amputating a foot."

16 – "Ciano's newspaper" was Il Telegrafo, the newspaper of Mussolini's son-in-law and, for a time, his foreign minister, Galeazzo Ciano

17 – Pierre Laval was chief minister in Vichy France and was executed in 1945

18 – Ioannis Metaxas served as prime minister of Greece from 1936 until his death in 1941

19 – *Bret Harte was an American writer renowned for his stories of Gold Rush-era California*

20 – *Graham Greene, Journey Without Maps (Vintage, 2006; first published by William Heinemann, 1936), P. 25/26*

21 – *The death of Miss Jane Margaret Houston was recorded in the January 1941 edition of The British Journal of Nursing. Under the title, "The Passing Bell", it read as follows: "It is with deep regret that we record the death on December 12th, 1940, on Active Service overseas, of Miss Jane Margaret Houston, Sister, Queen Alexandra's Imperial Military Nursing Service Reserve. Trained at the Glasgow Royal Infirmary, 1934-1939, Miss Houston was appointed Staff Nurse, Q.A.I.M.N.S. Reserve, on September 4th, 1939, and promoted Sister on September 4th, 1940. Miss Houston served in France with the British Expeditionary Force from September, 1939, to June, 1940, and later joined another hospital proceeding abroad. She was one of the younger members of the Reserve and her death will be keenly felt by her colleagues." Sister Houston is buried in Freetown's King Tom Cemetery.*

22 – *An extract from The Rubaiyat of Omar Khayyam*

23 – *Claude Houghton had a bit of a vogue when Jack was reading him – but few today will have heard of this well-respected but now-forgotten novelist*

24 – *The Daily Record, May 13, 1941*

25 – *"Bellum inferendum" translates as "I/We must make war on"*

26 – *Relates to A. E. Housman (1859–1936), an English poet and pre-eminent classicist*

27 – *John O'London's Weekly was a very popular literary magazine published between 1919 and 1954*

28 – *July 26 was his wedding anniversary. Jack and Betty's marriage lasted for 64-years*

29 – *"O di immortales O pisces minimi!" is a joking translation of the English expression, "Ye gods and little fishes"*

30 – *"Vox populi vox Dei" translates as "the voice of the people is the voice of God"*

31 – *Should perhaps read, "Vox populi vox sui Dei" – that is, "the voice of the people is the voice of their own God" or maybe even, "the voice of the people is the voice of the particular God they are following"*

32 – *Edwin Morgan, Thirteen Ways of Looking at Rillie (Enitharmon Press, 2006)*

33 – *The Herald, "Jack Rillie; university lecturer", December 3, 2009*

Glossary

157^(th) FA – *157^(th) Lowland Field Ambulance*
AA Guns – *Anti-Aircraft guns also known as Ack-Ack guns*
ADMS – *Assistant Director of Medical Services*
Bumboats – *Small boats used to ferry goods for sale to ships anchored offshore*
Cutter – *Small marine vessel used by naval services to carry light stores or passengers*
Davit – *Crane for raising and lowering equipment (such as lifeboats) on and off ships*
DO – *Dental Officer*
FA – *Field Ambulance*
FF – *Free French*
GBS – *George Bernard Shaw*
GOC – *General Officer Commanding*
HLI – *Highland Light Infantry*
IC – *Intelligence Corps*
KOSB – *The King's Own Scottish Borderers*
L/Cpl – *Lance Corporal*
MI – *Medical Inspection*
MO – *Medical Officer*
MT malaria – **Malignant Tertian malaria**
NCO – *Non-Commissioned Officer, e.g. sergeant*
ND – *Night Duty*
New-Cars – *Tramcars*
NYD – *Not Yet Diagnosed*
OC – *Officer Commanding*
Post-Cpl – *Corporal responsible for all mail arriving on base*
PT kit – *Physical Training kit*
QM – *Quartermaster. Officer with overall responsibility for supplies*
RASC – *Royal Army Service Corps: responsible for supplying petrol, general supplies, transport*
REME – *Royal Electrical and Mechanical Engineers*
RSM – *Regimental Sergeant Major*
SF – *Scarlet Fever*
SS – *Steamship*
S/Sgt – *Staff Sergeant*
Tender – *Boat used to ferry people and supplies to and from a ship*
Trichloroethylene – *Industrial solvent also used as an anaesthetic*
WOSB – *War Office Selection Board (officer cadet selection panel of British Army)*

Bibliography

BBC – History – The Battle of Britain. [Online]. (http://www.bbc.co.uk/history/battle_of_britain). (Accessed March 23, 2012)

BBC News – UK – Battle of Britain. [Online]. (http://news.bbc.co.uk/hi/english/static/in_depth/uk/2000/battle_of_britain/page01.stm). (Accessed March 23, 2012)

BBC On This Day 1940: Dunkirk rescue is over – Churchill defiant. [Online]. (http://news.bbc.co.uk/onthisday/hi/dates/stories/june/4/newsid_3500000/3500865.stm). (Accessed March 23, 2012)

Crowder, Michael, Colonial West Africa (Frank Cass and Company Limited, 1978)

Davies, Carole Boyce (ed.), Encyclopedia of the African Diaspora, Origins, Experiences, and Culture, (ABC-CLIO, Inc. 2008)

Dorman, Andrew M., Blair's Successful War, British Military Intervention in Sierra Leone (Ashgate Publishing Limited, 2009)

Education Scotland. [Online]. Clydebank Blitz. (http://www.educationscotland.gov.uk/scotlandshistory/20thand21stcenturies/worldwarII/clydebankblitz/index.asp). (Accessed March 5, 2014)

Fyfe, Christopher, A History of Sierra Leone (Oxford University Press, 1962)

Greene, Graham, The Heart of the Matter (Penguin Books, 1962; first published by William Heinemann, 1948)

Greene, Graham, Journey Without Maps (Vintage, 2006; first published by William Heinemann, 1936)

Harris, John, A Funny Place to Hold a War (Book Club Associates, 1984)

Jackson, Ashley, The British Empire and the Second World War (London: Continuum, 2006)

Jalloh, Alusine, The Fula Trading Diaspora in Colonial Sierra Leone, in The African Diaspora, ed. A. Jalloh and S. E. Maizlish (The University of Texas Press, 1996)

LeVert, Suzanne, Cultures of the World, Sierra Leone, (Marshall Cavendish International (Asia) Private Limited, 2006)

Livingstone, Thomas, Tommy's War, A First World War Diary (HarperPress, 2008)

McGonigal, James, Beyond the Last Dragon: A Life of Edwin Morgan (Sandstone Press Ltd, 2010)

McKendrick, Tom, Blitz, West Dunbartonshire Council. [Online]. (http://www.west-dunbarton.gov.uk/leisure-parks-events/tourism-and-visitor-attractions/museums-and-galleries/collections/war-and-military/blitz/). (Accessed March 5, 2014)

Morgan, Edwin, Thirteen Ways of Looking at Rillie (Enitharmon Press, 2006)

Overy, Professor Richard (February 17, 2011). [Online]. BBC – History – The

Soviet-German War 1941 – 1945. (http://www.bbc.co.uk/history/worldwars/ wwtwo/soviet_german_war_01.shtml). (Accessed March 23, 2012)

Sherwood, Marika (March 30, 2011). BBC – History – Colonies, Colonials and World War Two. [Online]. (http://www.bbc.co.uk/history/worldwars/wwtwo/ colonies_colonials_01.shtml). (Accessed March 23, 2012)

Singer, Barnett, Langdon, John W., Cultured Force, Makers and Defenders of the French Colonial Empire (The University of Wisconsin Press, 2004)

Stewart, Cameron (ed.), A Very Unimportant Officer, Life and Death on the Somme and at Passchendaele (Hodder & Stoughton, 2008)

Acknowledgements

To all those who helped make this special project a reality, my sincerest thanks.

But, thanks especially to my mother, Judith, and father, Ahmad, without whose unswerving generosity, patience, love and support this book would likely have never seen the light of day; to Marshall Walker, a life-long fan of Jack's, for his encouragement and invaluable advice; to Heather Faulkner and Marek Dalibor for kindly putting me up in their Freetown home, pointing me in the right direction and sharing their one and only bottle of Caol Ila; and lastly, to Eilidh, for her love, time and continued support and encouragement.

Others who accompanied me – knowingly or otherwise! – on this long journey include Andrew Hook, Alexander Maitland, Jim McCall, James McGonigal, the McLean family (for listening patiently to my never-ending updates), the staff of Glasgow's Mitchell Library, Mohammad (my helpful and congenial Freetown taxi driver/guide), John Mills (my much-appreciated Latin specialist), Professor Richard Rathbone (for talking all things West African) and Paul Sulzberger.

Excerpts from The Heart of the Matter and Journey Without Maps are reproduced by kind permission of David Higham Associates. William McIlvanney's quote from The Herald obituary of December 3, 2009, titled, "Jack Rillie; university lecturer", is reproduced by kind permission of Herald and Times Group. Excerpts from Edwin Morgan's poem Thirteen Ways of Looking at Rillie, and the 2004 image, are reproduced by kind permission of The Edwin Morgan Trust (SCIO).

Efforts have been made to contact copyright holders for material published in this book. If any owner has been inadvertently overlooked, then the publisher would be glad to hear from them and make good in future editions any omissions brought to their attention.

Photograph Credits

The photographs are from those in Jack's personal possession, with the following exceptions. Wherever possible, permission has been sought. Grateful thanks to the following for permission to reproduce:

Jack, Gold Coast, c.1944-45: Alex Osei, Alex Photographic Studio

Jack holding court at his beloved University of Glasgow, c.1975: Photographic Unit, University of Glasgow

U.S. Army Map Service, Freetown, 1942: Courtesy of the University of Texas Libraries, The University of Texas at Austin

Monarch of Bermuda: B. and A. Feilden/J. and M. Clarkson

The ruins of old Fourah Bay College – constructed between 1845 and 1848 – in Cline Town, Freetown, today: Alasdair Soussi

Looking out over the red roofs of Freetown today: Alasdair Soussi

A street-level view of Freetown's legendary Cotton Tree: Christian Trede, distributed under a CC BY-SA 2.0 DE license

Sister Houston is buried at Freetown's King Tom Cemetery: The War Graves Photographic Project

The war graves at Freetown's King Tom Cemetery: The War Graves Photographic Project

A street scene of Second World War Freetown, November 7, 1942: John Atherton, distributed under a CC BY-SA 2.0 license

Jack reading Thirteen Ways of Looking at Rillie, *Clarence Court, Glasgow, 2004*: Alan Riach

About the Editor

Scots-born Alasdair Soussi is an internationally-published freelance journalist, with a special interest in the Middle East and the Islamic world, and the Scottish political scene.

From features on Cairo's street children, Britain's forced marriage victims, the Lockerbie tragedy and Sierra Leone's amputees to profiles of Howard Carter, T.E. Lawrence and Sir Wilfred Thesiger, his work has appeared in Al Jazeera English, ASPIRE magazine, BBC online, The Guardian, The Herald, The Irish Times, Macleans, The National, Sunday Herald *and* The Weekly Standard.

alasdairsoussi.com.
@AlasdairSoussi

Lightning Source UK Ltd.
Milton Keynes UK
UKOW07f2044171214

243317UK00020B/463/P